# The Great Plague and Great Fire of London: The History and Legacy of England's Most Famous Disasters of the 17th Century

## By Charles River Editors

A medieval illustration depicting people with the plague being blessed

## About Charles River Editors

**Charles River Editors** is a boutique digital publishing company, specializing in bringing history back to life with educational and engaging books on a wide range of topics. Keep up to date with our new and free offerings with [this 5 second sign up on our weekly mailing list](), and visit [Our Kindle Author Page]() to see other recently published Kindle titles.

We make these books for you and always want to know our readers' opinions, so we encourage you to leave reviews and look forward to publishing new and exciting titles each week.

# Introduction

# The Great Plague of London

**A medieval depiction of plague victims being buried**

"The trend of recent research is pointing to a figure more like 45–50% of the European population dying during a four-year period. There is a fair amount of geographic variation. In Mediterranean Europe, areas such as Italy, the south of France and Spain, where plague ran for about four years consecutively, it was probably closer to 75–80% of the population. In Germany and England ... it was probably closer to 20%." - Philip Daileader, medieval historian

In the 14th century, a ruthless killer stalked the streets of England, wiping out up to 60% of the terror-stricken nation's inhabitants. This invisible and unforgiving terminator continued to harass the population for hundreds of years, but nothing could compare to the savagery it would unleash 3 centuries later. This conscienceless menace was none other than the notorious bubonic plague, also known as the "Black Death."

The High Middle Ages had seen a rise in Western Europe's population in previous centuries, but these gains were almost entirely erased as the plague spread rapidly across all of Europe from 1346-1353. With a medieval understanding of medicine, diagnosis, and illness, nobody understood what caused Black Death or how to truly treat it. As a result, many religious people assumed it was divine retribution, while superstitious and suspicious citizens saw a nefarious human plot involved and persecuted certain minority groups among them.

Though it is now widely believed that rats and fleas spread the disease by carrying the bubonic plague westward along well-established trade routes, and there are now vaccines to prevent the spread of the plague, the Black Death gruesomely killed upwards of 100 million people, with helpless chroniclers graphically describing the various stages of the disease. It took Europe decades for its population to bounce back, and similar plagues would affect various parts of the world for the next several centuries, but advances in medical technology have since allowed researchers to read various medieval accounts of the Black Death in order to understand the various strains of the disease. Furthermore, the social upheaval caused by the plague radically changed European societies, and some have noted that by the time the plague had passed, the Late Middle Ages would end with many of today's European nations firmly established.

In the mid-17th century, the heart of England fell victim to the mother of all epidemic catastrophes. The city of London was a ghost town, deserted by those who knew better than to hang around in a breeding ground that offered near-certain doom. Those who were confined within the city's borders had to make do with what they had, and the pitifully low morale seemed appropriate; the reek of rot and decomposition pervaded the air day in and day out, while corpses, young and old, riddled with strange swellings and blackened boils, littered the streets. For Londoners, to say it was hell would be an understatement.

*The Great Plague and Great Fire of London: The History and Legacy of England's Most Famous Disasters of the 17th Century* explores the horrific disasters, their origins, the peculiar precautions and curious cures designed to combat them, and the sobering legacies they left behind. Along with pictures depicting important people, places, and events, you will learn about the Great Plague and Great Fire of London like never before.

## The Great Fire of London (September 2-5, 1666)

*The third day of The Great Fire of London September 4 1666*

"[A] wooden, northern, and inartificial congestion of Houses." – John Evelyn's description of London before the fire

"So I was called for, and did tell the King and Duke of York what I saw, and that unless His Majesty did command houses to be pulled down nothing could stop the fire. They seemed much troubled, and the King commanded me to go to my Lord Mayor from him, and command him to spare no houses, but to pull down before the fire every way." – Samuel Pepys

In the 17th century, the people of London could boast that they had developed some of the most advanced firefighting technology and methods in the world, including the use of primitive fire engines. There were even vendors of such machines who advertised in papers of their machines' abilities to quench great fires. Of course, even with trained firefighters and new devices, the most skillful efforts could still prove limited in the face of a giant fire, as Rome had learned over 1500 years earlier and as Chicago would learn nearly 200 years later.

In fact, one of the primary reasons London developed ways to fight fires was the fact that the city was particularly vulnerable. Although London was over 1500 years old and sat at the heart of the British Empire, most of the buildings were made of wood, and the city was overcrowded, in part due to the fact that city planners worked with and around the ancient Roman fortifications that had been constructed to defend it. As such, while there were spacious areas for the elite and rich outside of the city, London itself had narrow streets full of wood buildings that were practically on top of each other.

With some bad luck and bad timing, a potential disaster awaited the city, and that finally came in September 1666. As it turned out, the Great Fire of London was so bad that one author who studied the blaze described it as "the perfect fire," referring to the convergence in the largest city in England of spark, wood and wind in such a way that no one could stop the fire or even fight it effectively. John Evelyn, who had warned of the potential for a devastating fire given the layout of the city, noted that people seemed so stunned by the scope of the fire that they didn't know what to do: "The conflagration was so universal, and the people so astonished, that from the beginning, I know not by what despondency or fate, they hardly stirred to quench it, so that there was nothing heard or seen but crying out and lamentation, running about like distracted creatures without at all attempting to save even their goods, such a strange consternation there was upon them."

While the fire quickly spread throughout the heart of the city, the only thing that saved London's suburbs was an ancient wall built around the city to keep the enemies of Rome out, not the fire in. By the time it was finished, most of the city's homes and churches lay in ashes, and nearly 90% of the city's citizens were left homeless. The only consolation taken away from the devastation was an astonishing low death rate; although London had about 80,000 residents, only a handful died as the fire raged across the city.

The fire lasted three days, and by the end of it, Londoners were shocked by the wide-scale destruction, which was so great that Samuel Pepys remarked, "It made me weep to see it." In the aftermath, people looked for scapegoats, ranging from King Charles II to the Pope and his Catholic supporters, while England's leaders looked to rebuild the city. The civil and foreign strife ultimately posed obstacles to new plans to rebuild London, which actually meant that the rebuilding efforts were designed in ways that mimicked the old layout that had invited such a disaster in the first place. Nonetheless, London never suffered a similar event, with the exception of German air raids during World War II.

The Great Plague and Great Fire of London: The History and Legacy of England's Most Famous Disasters of the 17th Century

About Charles River Editors

Introduction

The Great Plague

   The Black Death

   The Roots of the Plague

   A Familiar Chaos

   Therapy

   The Peak

   A Storm Weathered and a Winter's Thaw

The Great Fire

   Chapter 1: A Sad and Lamentable Accident

   Chapter 2: A Violent Easterly Wind Fomented It

   Chapter 3: Down the Hill to the Bridge

   Chapter 4: Members of the City

   Chapter 5: About the Tower

   Chapter 6: We Began to Hope Well

   Chapter 7: Disaffection at Home

   Chapter 8: Most Happily Mastered It

   Chapter 9: Very Great Loss

   Online Resources

   Bibliography

Free Books by Charles River Editors

Discounted Books by Charles River Editors

# The Great Plague

**The Black Death**

"Ring around a rosie, a pocket full of posies. Ashes, ashes, we all fall down." Oftentimes, giddy children can be seen belting out this jaunty, easily recognizable Mother Goose nursery rhyme, their hands linked as they dance around in a circle. As soon as the last word is uttered, the breathless children collapse in a fit of giggles. Bearing this in mind, many have since suggested that this iconic nursery rhyme is inlaid with nefarious undertones, and originated from even darker beginnings. According to a few chin-strokers, this seemingly innocent ditty was written as a morbid tribute to the merciless plague that ravaged Europe in the Middle Ages, lasting well into the 17th century.

Every line of the rhyme has since been dissected and extensively analyzed. For starters, a "rosie" referred to the middle portion of the back of one's hand, or the smooth space between one's wrist and fingers. Thusly, "ring around the rosie" was thought to be a romanticized description of the "rosie-red" or violet-tinged patches of rashes that appeared on the skin. This was one of the first tell-tale signs of the bubonic plague.

A "posie" was an old-fashioned term for "flower." This was said to describe the sprigs of flowers people had uprooted and either stuffed into their clothes or inhaled throughout the day, both a cost-effective and superstitious approach to staving off the disease. Others say it was used to mask the putrid scent of death from the mountains of disease-riddled bodies everywhere.

The definition behind the second line of the rhyme was varied. Some said it represented the flowers the dead were buried with, or had placed on their graves. There were also those who regarded the line as a visual depiction of the gut-churning pus that accumulated within the sores of the sick.

The "ashes" in the song signified the remnants of the diseased bodies, which were set ablaze to prevent the mysterious disease from multiplying. The ashes could also have signified the debris that remained from the houses that were torched to the ground, which had been ordered in response to the plague. In another version of the rhyme, "ashes" is replaced with "a-tishoo," the onomatopoeic term for a sneeze, and another common symptom of a certain strain of plague. Lastly, the final line of the rhyme and cue to the children's playful tumble to the ground was a reference to the swift and almost certain death that befell the ill-fated who were infected by the swift-acting contagion.

Today, theories of hidden meanings behind the nursery rhyme have generally been flushed down the drain by many historians, as well as the online myth-buster, *Snopes*. The rhyme first debuted in print in 1881, seen in *Mother Goose or the Old Nursery Rhymes*. Rumors suggested that the rhyme had been sung by children generation after generation since Europe's first tango with the plague, but there has been no record of the rhyme prior to the 1881 publication.

Multiple versions of the song were soon published thereafter. One alteration read, "Round the ring of roses, pots full of posies, the one stoops the last, shall tell whom she loves best." Another version recounts the posies being distributed to characters named Jim, Jack, and Moses. Contrarians hope to nip these theories in the bud, and have concluded that these versions, which clearly have nothing to do with death or disease, are simply a nonsensical song meant for the playground.

Nonetheless, what is certain is that the plague was a monstrous malady caused by the bacterium, *yersinia pestis*. The microscopic but lethal entity was usually fostered in the nests of wild rodents in sewers, streets, alleyways, and the squalid homes of the poor, and was believed to have multiplied with each furry body. Scientists today have coined names for these hotbeds of diseases – "plague reservoirs," or "plague focuses."

The plague comes in 3 strains – the septicemic, the pneumonic, and the bubonic. The septicemic plague is spawned when the aforementioned bacteria finds its way into the victim's bloodstream. The pneumonic is the deadliest of all the strains, as it seizes control of one's lungs. The invisible bacteria ejected from an ostensibly small cough or sneeze is enough to transmit the contagion to the next healthy person.

However, the most notorious strain is the bubonic plague, the first phase and most commonly contracted type of this disease. For many years, scientists have believed that the Black Death was a form of the bubonic plague, a deadly illness carried and spread by fleas found on rodents. The belief was that rats covered with the fleas traveled west on boats to Europe, where they reproduced and spread their infected parasites to humans, who subsequently contracted the plague and died. However, given the different strains and symptoms found across Europe, it has been alternatively suggested that the Black Death that attacked Europe during the 1340s and 1350s might also have been caused by an airborne pathogen of some sort, and this was certainly the belief that those afraid of the disease embraced. Gabriele de' Mussis, a lawyer in Piacenza during the Middle Ages, noted, "As it happened, among those who escaped from Caffa by boat were a few sailors who had been infected with the poisonous disease. Some boats were bound for Genoa, others went to Venice and to other Christian areas. When the sailors reached these palaces and mixed with the people there, it was as if they had brought evil spirits with them: every city, every settlement, every places was poisoned by the contagious pestilence, and their inhabitants, both men and women, died suddenly. And when one person had contracted the illness, he poisoned his whole family even as he fell and died, so that those preparing to bury his body were seized by death in the same way. Thus death entered through the windows, and as cities and towns were depopulated their inhabitants mourned their dead neighbors." Cortusii Patavini Duo, who wrote from Padua, recorded similar thoughts: "After which the unprecedented plague crossed the sea and so came to the Veneto, Lombardy, the March, Tuscany, Germany,

France and spread through virtually the whole world. It was carried by some infected people who travelled from the East and who, by sight alone, or by touch, by breathing on them, killed everyone. The infection was incurable; it could not be avoided."

One of the things that made the plague seem to be some form of divine retribution is that it did indeed appear to have arrived from the East, a place the European Catholics considered pagan. Today it's apparent that the disease was not the result of an evil plot put together by the enemies of Christianity but almost certainly carried by rats infested with fleas. Still, many sailors returning to Europe from voyages to either Asia or the Middle East likely did bring the sickness with them, a fact that Mussis pointed out: "Thus almost everyone who had been in the East, or in the regions to the south and north, fell victim to sudden death after contracting this pestilential disease, as if struck by lethal arrow which raised a tumor on their bodies. The scale of the mortality and the form which it too persuaded those who lived, weeping and lamenting, through the bitter events of 1346 to 1348—the Chinese, Indians, Persians, Medes, Kurds, Armenians, Cilicians, Georgians, Mesopotamians, Nubians, Ethiopians, Turks, Egyptians, Arabs, Saracens and Greeks (for almost all the East had been affected)—that the last judgment had come."

While people struggled to explain the plague back then, today it is known that the plague is typically contracted by a pest, usually a rodent or a flea. In the most extreme cases, this brand of the disease can be incurred through the mere touch of an infected person's clothing. If untreated, which it almost always was, the disease would branch out to the blood or the lungs, which prompted the next phases of septicemic or pneumonic plague, respectively.

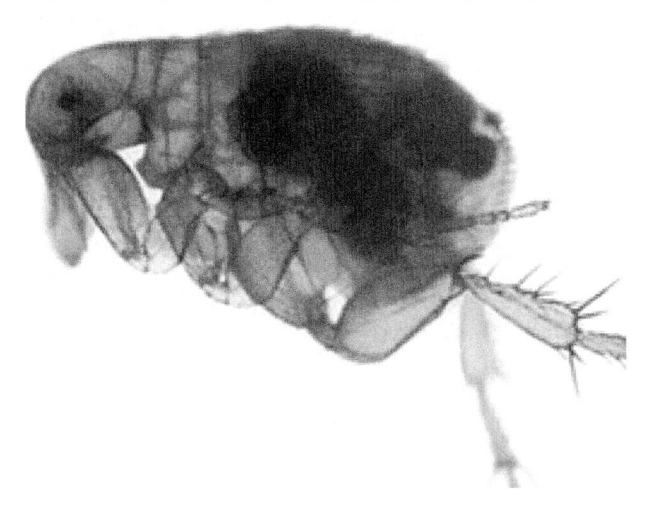

Actual size ⟶

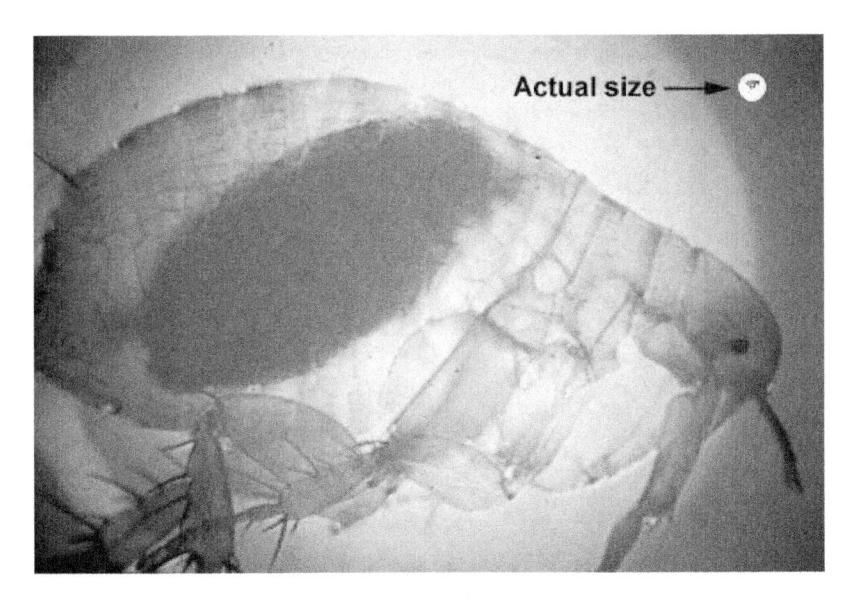

**Microscopic views of Oriental rat fleas**

These days, when confronted with a mouse camping out behind a crack in the wall, or snacking on a treat in one's kitchen cupboard, most would squeal, make a snatch for the broom, and sweep them out the back door. In places with serious rodent infestations, people today often install mouse traps or resort to rodenticides to shoo away these pests, but back in the day, these privileges were far beyond the public's reach.

The disease was typically hosted by black rats, otherwise known as "ship rats" or "house rats." These critters were unlike the gray or brown rodents that frequented the nooks and crannies of cellars and sewers, often scurrying away at the sound of an approaching human's footsteps. It was precisely the black rat's habit of residing close to humans that made them such a menace to the public.

On average, it took about 10-14 days for a colony of the bacteria-infested rats to die out, but the decomposing rodents naturally attracted another swarm of fleas, on top of those that had already made permanent residence within the fur of these rats. These fleas, new and old, would become contaminated. Once the blood in these rodent corpses had been fully drained, the fleas would have no choice but to hunt for new hosts.

Infected fleas often set their targets on unsuspecting humans. Then, these fleas sunk their triple-probe mouth parts into the dirt-caked flesh of humans, most often dining in one's neck, armpit, groin, or thigh. Within a span of 3-5 days, the small, smarting bite would have ballooned into a tender, throbbing lymph node, known as a bubo, a term that later motivated the christening of the strain. When the infection had set in, the diseased faced an 80% mortality rate. From start to finish, their roller-coaster towards death came to a screeching halt in roughly 23 days. Apart from rats, other rumored carriers of the disease were cats, rabbits, squirrels, chipmunks, prairie dogs, and even house-broken pets.

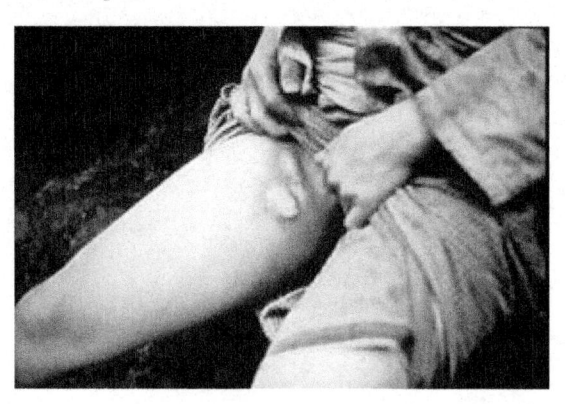

**A victim of the bubonic plague with swollen lymph nodes visible**

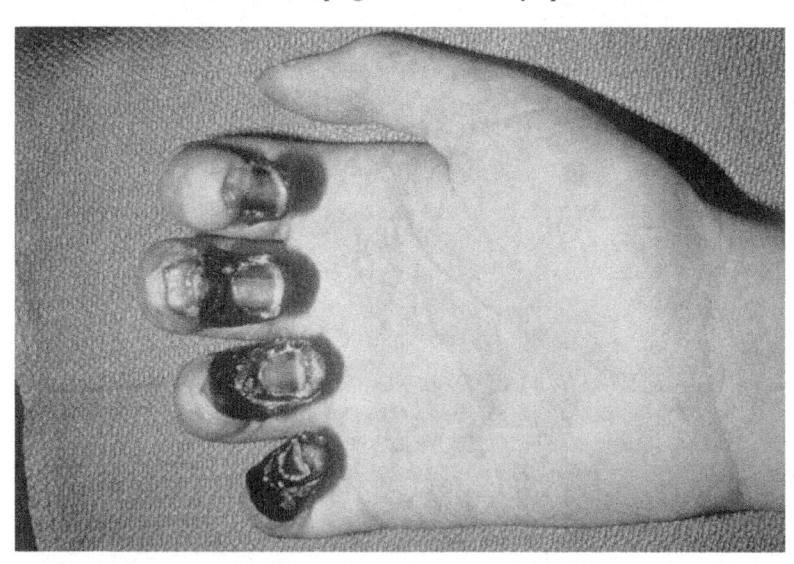

**A victim of the bubonic plague with fingers blackened by the illness**

By the 17th century, the plague was a familiar anomaly to the people of Europe, for it was anything but their first kiss with the debilitating disease. The earliest case in Europe was reported to have occurred in Messina, Sicily, in October of 1347. A fleet of a dozen Genoese trading ships from the Crimean region were docked at the Sicilian harbor, seemingly taking a brief respite after lengthy and turbulent travels through the Black Sea. As they were expected to have embarked upon a trading route that took them past Constantinople, through the glittering green heart of the Mediterranean Seas and into China, the townspeople were excited to hear their exotic tales, and steal a peek at the porcelain, silk, and tea brought back from faraway lands. Crowds gathered around the ships to welcome the travelers, waving, cheering, and offering them well wishes. But this cheering soon petered out when the visitors noticed how strangely still these ships were. Not a single soul had come out to meet them. Spooked, a band of men dispatched from the local authorities boarded the ships to investigate the uncanny silence, only to be greeted by a hideous sight. In all 12 ships, all the crewmen were either slumped over against wayward furniture, or sprawled out across the floors. Most of them were ice-cold and perfectly rigid. Only a fraction remained breathing, but just barely.

More sweat coursed down the rattled investigators' necks when they saw that all the sailors exhibited the same eerie symptoms. Those clinging onto their last breaths were curled up in a ball, or doubled over in excruciating pain, their lips chalky-white, but their faces and skin hot to the touch. Most alarming of all were the ghastly black boils that had sprouted from these men's bodies, pulsing and oozing a nauseating mixture of pus and blood. These men rolled around, delirious, hallucinating, and clearly dehydrated, but what food and water they could manage immediately shot back out of them. It was these very boils that would give this dreadful condition its nickname – "black death."

It did not take long for the locals of Messina to realize the gravity of having readily invited a little-known but clearly deadly disease into their land. They quickly shunned the ships from the port, but the damage was already done. The plague spread through the city like an uncontainable wildfire. A great number of those who had been stricken tried to escape and sought refuge in the countryside, but that only carried the disease into rural Messina.

Pandemonium would not be a strong enough term to describe the chaos that had erupted. By the next month, the so-called "death ships" that were thrust back into sea were said to have randomly steered themselves into the docks of the Mediterranean islands of Sardinia, an autonomous region of Italy, and Corsica of France. Tana, a trading post in Genoa, Italy, became another breeding ground for the plague. The unforeseen outbreak was grave enough to interrupt a conflict between the Christian merchants and the Tatars, the latter a Muslim Turkic people who had taken control of the Christian stronghold in the Crimean city of Caffa.

Today, the short-lived invasion is known as the "Siege of Caffa," which was said to have featured one of the earliest instances of biological warfare. When the plague struck, the Tatars were forced to retreat, lest they be infected. Before doing so, they launched plague-claimed corpses over the wall in a last-ditch attempt to infect the residents. The citizens of Caffa hustled to fling these corpses out into sea, but the damage had been done. Thousands fell ill and later succumbed to the disease. A few attempted to book it, boarding ships and setting sail for neighboring countries. In the process, many of them unwittingly become carriers of the disease.

That was all it took for the plague to continue spreading. That year, only a few regions in Italy and Greece would feel the wrath of the plague, but that would soon change. In just another 6 months, about half the continent had been affected by the plague. Those in Marseilles, France, as well as Valencia and Barcelona of Spain, would meet a similar fate to those at Messina.

The plague was as ruthless as it was unstoppable. The absence of a proper international, or even cross-continental communication system made it even more difficult for the stricken cities to sound the alarm bells in time. In the months that followed, the disease with no bias seeped into the borders of Germany, as well as certain regions of Africa and the Middle East.

Italy ranked close to the top of the doom list. The plague had spread from Genoa to Tuscany, and from there to Florence, Siena, Rome, and Avignon, the papal city at the time. Florence suffered one of the worst mortality rates, seeing 100,000 of its inhabitants wiped out in the span of 4 months. In certain neighboring cities, the plague was said to have killed up to 90% of their residents.

When the disease reached Milan, authorities there were one of the first to enact preventative measures. As soon as the pestilence made an appearance in the city, claiming the inhabitants of the first 3 houses, said houses were instantly quarantined. Under instruction of the Milanese archbishop, the afflicted were locked in and kept under medieval house arrest, where they were essentially left with no other option but to await their impending deaths. As cold-blooded as the measure might seem, it appeared to be the only viable option in a panicking and primitive climate. It also seemed to bear fruit to some extent, as the city's mortality rates were visibly lower than those of their neighbors.

The streets of Florence experienced one of the most deafening silences, losing 65,000 of its citizens. Giovanni Boccaccio, author of *The Decameron*, painted a haunting picture of the scene: "In the year of our Lord 1348...in Florence, the finest city in all of Italy, a most terrible plague...Men and women in great numbers left the city, their houses, relations, and effects, and tied into the country...concluding that none ought to stay in a place thus doomed to destruction."

A depiction of the plague in Florence as described by *The Decameron*

**A medieval depiction of Boccaccio and other Florentines fleeing the plague**

In the city of Siena, the disease was taking a flagrant toll on everyday business. Construction on a cathedral ceased the moment the contractors were gusted with the frigid wind of disease. Funds for the project had to be diverted to the aid of the ill workers. Ultimately, the project was scrapped and the site left abandoned. It can still be found today, serving as a chilling reminder of the historic plague.

During this time, a group of God-fearing vigilantes took matters into their own hands. These men maintained a widely-held belief that the plague was a product of God's anger. Collectively known as the "Brotherhood of the Flagellants," the brothers marched through the cities of Europe, their pleading prayers ringing across the gloomy streets as they lashed at themselves with thorny scourges. At times, they invited passersby to join in on the act, a perfect example of the testament to the desperation of the tainted cities.

Over the next 5 years, an estimated 20-30 million perished in Europe alone. This sobering statistic would one day lead chroniclers to describe the event as the "medieval equivalent of a nuclear holocaust." As the plague secured most of the trade routes, avoiding the plague was next to impossible. The southern tip of England was infected as early as June of 1348, and by the next year, the disease had made its way through the rest of Great Britain.

Due to their limited knowledge of medicine, and the almost total lack of any reliable method of studying and treating disease, there were no verifiable ways known to avoid contracting the disease. As such, rumors began to spread abundantly. Louis Heyligen, a musician serving Cardinal Giovanni Colonna, hoped that maybe he had learned something while working in the papal court that could save his friends. In a letter, he wrote, "I am writing to you, most dearly beloved, so that you should know in what perils we are now living. And if you wish to preserve yourselves, the best advice is that a man should eat and drink moderately, and avoid getting cold, and refrain from any excess, and above all mix little with people—unless it be with a few who have healthy breath; but it is best to stay at home until the epidemic has passed. According to astrologers the epidemic takes ten years to complete its cycle, of which three have now elapsed, and so it is to be feared that in the end it will have encircled the whole world, although they say that it will affect the cold region more slowly."

On the other hand, Giovanni Boccaccio had his own ideas about what would prevent one from catching the plague, though since he was neither a doctor nor a scientist, his ideas were more of a hopeful collection of rumors going around than any sort of definitive advice. He wrote, "Some thought that moderate living and the avoidance of all superfluity would preserve them from the epidemic. They formed small communities, living entirely separate from everybody else. They shut themselves up in houses where there were no sick, eating the finest food and drinking the best wine very temperately, avoiding all excess, allowing no news or discussion of death and sickness, and passing the time in music and suchlike pleasures. Others thought just the opposite. They thought the sure cure for the plague was to drink and be merry, to go about singing and amusing themselves, satisfying every appetite they could, laughing and jesting at what happened. They put their words into practice, spent day and night going from tavern to tavern, drinking immoderately, or went into other people's houses, doing only those things which pleased them. This they could easily do because everyone felt doomed and had abandoned his property, so that most houses became common property and any stranger who went in made use of them as if he had owned them. And with all this bestial behavior, they avoided the sick as much as possible.

... Many others adopted a course of life midway between the two just described. They did not restrict their victuals so much as the former, nor allow themselves to be drunken and dissolute like the latter, but satisfied their appetites moderately. They did not shut themselves up, but went about, carrying flowers or scented herbs or perfumes in their hands, in the belief that it was an excellent thing to comfort the brain with such odors; for the whole air was infected with the smell of dead bodies, of sick persons and medicines."

There were a few portions of Europe that succeeded in avoiding the plague. Milan's brutal preventative measures proved effective, and it emerged as one of the cities with the lowest plague-induced mortality rates. Southern France, one of the lesser populated areas, as well as the port city of Bruges, managed to escape relatively unscathed.

Be that as it may, the plague would not stay away. Mass outbreaks would be resurrected, targeting different cities every couple of decades. It struck London again in 1349, where the city experienced nearly 3 consecutive outbreaks in the same year. Then, it revisited Paris in 1466, where 40,000 died in the city itself. In 1497, it would be Barcelona that was affected. Between the first plague pandemic and 1497, Barcelona, along with the Catalonian region, underwent a drastic shrink in population, with the census dropping from an estimated 600,000 to 278,000.

The plague persisted into the next century, ravaging Madrid in 1506, and Seville a few years prior, which claimed up to 700,000 lives. In 1550, the disease cut the population of York in half. Even Milan, which had succeeded in dodging the plague for so long, could not hold on much longer. In 1630, about 150,000 of its 200,000-250,000 inhabitants were no more.

**An early 15th century Bible's illustration believed to depict the plague**

That said, it seemed that none could compare to England, as the nation appeared to be an inauspicious magnet for the miserable disease. Following its first strike in the 14th century, the problem reached such a dire status that mass graves had to be shoveled out of the ground to accommodate the countless bodies. The city of London suffered a couple more times closely after, once in 1563, and then again in 1625.

The plague had become such a regular occurrence that authorities scrambled to contain the situation with laws, regulations, and decrees. In 1518, the first regulations were installed in London, requiring its citizens to hang a bundle of straw outside their door to signify an infected house. The infected would then be boxed into their homes for a period of 40 days. The infected were also tasked with carrying sticks dipped in white paint in the rare occasion they were allowed in public, so that others would know to keep their distance. The disease continued to linger, which resulted in more seemingly futile regulations.

In the summer of 1644, a fresh outbreak in Oxford, home to the king, reanimated the panic. More quarantines, as well as the mass slaying of cats and dogs, both wild and domesticated, were ordered. In Newark, guards were stationed by the doors of the quarantined homes, which did nothing to slow down the plague's effects. By 1646, following another 1,000 recorded deaths, Newark was labeled "a miserable stinking infected town." In the next year, another 3,597 plague-related deaths were recorded in London. As macabre as the figure sounds today, to the 17th century Londoners, this was a good year.

For reasons undisclosed to the residents, the city of London seemed to have been dealt one of the worst hands in the country – perhaps all of the continent. Time and time again, the city had been smitten with returning epidemics. In 1603, the plague claimed 30,000 lives. 22 years later, that number was bumped up to 35,000. Later on, Londoners were granted a glimpse of hope as that number dropped to 10,000 in 1636, and it continued to sink steadily lower after that. Londoners hoped that the dwindling mortality rates signified the dawn of a better day. Much to their consternation, it would be anything but.

One cold winter night in 1664, a bright, fiery comet hurtled across the inky night sky. This, the gasping witnesses believed, was an omen of doom and destruction. As it turned out, the worst epidemic was indeed lurking on the horizon.

**The Roots of the Plague**

"How many valiant men, how many fair ladies, breakfast with their kinfolk and the same night supped with their ancestors in the next world...Many died in the open street, others dying in their houses, made it known by the stench of their rotting bodies." – Giovanni Boccaccio

Even to this day, the origins of the Black Death are disputed. A wide range of historians have suspected and named China, India, Mongolia, as well as other parts of central Asia and southern Russia as the source of the crippling disease. While documents from the 14th century have presented theories relating to the disease's eastern origins, modern historians take this fact with a grain of salt, as none of these were first-hand accounts.

One of the most popular theories of origin blames China as the source of the plague, apparently making its first appearance over 2,600 years ago. These "oriental rat fleas" not only hitched a ride on critters that journeyed across the Silk Road, they became unwanted passengers on trading vessels. From that point forward, the disease was said to have bled into Western Europe around the 14th century, and later, to Africa. When the plague was introduced to the United States through Hawaii 500 years later, fingers were once again pointed at China.

In the early 2000s, archaeologist Eva Panagiotakopulu from the University of Sheffield, England, challenged this theory. The fossil expert declared that the plague had originated in Egypt, and she claimed that she had found archaeological evidence to support her theory. These findings had been discovered by chance during a routine excavation that aimed to learn more about the daily life of Egyptians 3 millennia ago. The dried up insects unearthed at the site, Panagiotakopulu insisted, were her golden clues. While sifting through the ruins of what had once been the homes of pharaoh tomb-makers, she had come upon the remains of both cat and human fleas. Mummified rats later found by the Nile Delta added weight to this theory. Most intriguing of all, ancient medical writings from a document entitled "Ebers Papyrus," circa 1500 BCE, described an all-too-familiar disease, one that "produced a bubo, and pus that [has] petrified."

The first of the 3 plague pandemics to come is now referred to as the "Justinian Plague," as it had occurred during the era of Byzantine Emperor Justinian the Great's reign (527-565). The first case of the destructive disease was recorded in Pelusium in the year 541, a city in Egypt's Nile Delta. Others claim the disease had made its first waves a year earlier in Ethiopia. From Pelusium, the plague split east and west, heading to the densely populated cities of Palestine and Alexandria.

By 544, the disease, which saw its victims conquered by buboes and septicemia, had penetrated the borders of the African Tunisia, and Italy. For the next 2 centuries, the areas of what would become England and Ireland, as well as the Sahara, Iberian Peninsula, Persia, and other stretches of east Asia would have their first encounters with the calamity. Between the years of 541 and 749, there were at least 17 different outbreaks around the globe.

Procopius of Caesarea, a Byzantine court chronicler, portrayed the plague as one powerful enough that the "whole human race came near to be annihilated." Excerpts from his book, *History of the Wars,* exhibited a vivid image of the events: "[The ill] were seized by the disease without becoming aware of what was coming, either through a waking vision or dream...They had sudden fever, some when just roused from sleep, others while walking about, and others while otherwise engaged, without any regard to what they were doing...In others on the following day, and in the rest not many days later, a bubonic swelling developed."

Not surprisingly, the mortality rates during the time are inconclusive. Between 541 and 544, the death toll had been placed at anywhere between 5,000-10,000. In Constantinople, home to Emperor Justinian, the plague victims died daily, claiming up to 300,000 lives at the end of its course. These virulent attacks and their frequent comebacks were rightly classified as "pandemics," as they affected a large portion of the world in a chain of cyclic infections.

But what could have brought about the second and third pandemics? The deplorable hygiene and sanitary conditions from the days of yore are believed to have been the chief contributors to the birth of the disease. Medieval sanitation in European cities, as opposed to the countryside, was especially abhorrent, due to its congested and poorly engineered towns, many of which were overrun by overpopulation. In a matter of 60 years, the number of citizens had tripled, with over half a million residents sandwiched within the city walls.

Rivers were not only a means of transportation, but served as the foundation for all basic necessities of the time. This was not only where the townspeople bathed, but where waste and garbage were disposed. Even so, people habitually filled their pails with the filthy river water, and, in a twist that would make modern health inspectors faint, they later used the water for cooking and drinking. The only semblance of a plumbing system consisted of the crude ditches and sewers that emptied out into the rivers.

In London, sanitary conditions were just as atrocious. Even in the homes of the wealthy, grimy chamber pots were stowed under beds for easy access to the toilet during the middle of the night. It is said that the British slang term for bathroom, "loo," had been birthed from the French term "*guardez le' eau*," which translates to "watch out for the water." Additionally, dirty leaves or moss were used as toilet paper.

Medieval Europeans were known for dumping their garbage and the contents of their chamber pots straight out of their windows and into the streets. Of course, before doing so, common etiquette required a trio of warning cries, so those outside could duck from the incoming splash in time. Some who had the room used chamber pots, and attached small rooms as an extension to their outermost walls on the second floor instead. There, a hole was punched into the ground of the private loo, designed so the user's waste flowed (or plopped) right into the alley or street below. Cesspits, which were holes dug out of the earth on their property, served as bathrooms for the poor. These were supposed to be regularly emptied, but this was rarely done.

Apart from the stream of excrement teeming through the town, the streets doubled as a landfill. Daily loads of garbage, along with entrails and discarded parts from the butcher shops, were also tossed out into the streets. Oftentimes, the blood-infused river of sewage spilled into the homes and nearby establishments around the butcher shops. To combat the rapidly mounting waste, townspeople relied on hungry animals and a rinse from the skies to drive the worst of the waste out of town.

In time, new technology and innovations sought to rectify the towns' hazardous conditions, but the tremendous ignorance of science made this an unachievable dream. This was a time when people were more than happy to apply leaded makeup to their faces, and swipe toxic powders and creams across their lips and eyelids. Scorching-hot pokers and leeches were the only available solutions for disinfecting a wound.

Beds were inhabited by bugs, pests, and at times, bird droppings, as most homes were built without roofs. Laundry detergent in ancient Rome consisted of lye made of ashes and urine, and even then, it was sparingly used. Medieval folk did not change their clothes, hats, or lice-infested wigs for months on end, as many believed that bathing was bad for one's health, a myth propagated by King James VI of Scotland himself.

**King James VI of Scotland and I of England**

By the time England had entered the 17th century, hygiene was no different, and in fact, some might say, was arguably worse. Though a hefty fine of 2 shillings had been placed upon those who were caught chucking garbage or excrement into the streets, few took heed of the new law. As pavements did not yet exist, people walked on the naked earth – in reality, the seemingly breathing tons of excrement, blood, and waste running through the winding streets. City sweepers, or "muck-rakers," were entrusted with scraping the filth off the streets, and since it was a job no one wanted, they were paid quite handsomely. The job was made even more unappealing by the fact that medieval Londoners and animals were said to have produced up to 50 tons of excrement every single day.

In poorer neighborhoods, sanitation was particularly difficult to police. Muck-rakers avoided the cities like the very disease that tormented them. As a result, the ground was constantly thick and slippery with waste and rotting carcasses, reeling in armies of resident flies and insects. When muck-rakers braved these neighborhoods, the waste from these cities would only be swept outside the city walls, where separate mounds of months' old waste were left to spoil even further. Day in and day out, people swerved out of the way to avoid getting drenched by irresponsible homeowners from the floors above, as well as the puddle splashes from carriages and horses whisking through the streets.

People did what they could to tolerate the noxious funk in the air. They walked around with handkerchiefs or "nosegays," which were satchels of flowers pressed firmly against their noses. The thick billows of black smoke coughing out of the 15,000 coal houses, along with the factories and breweries, made breathing even more challenging. Immigrants who had flooded the city in recent years had taken over massive tenements, which became vandalized, decrepit, and sordid, luring in even more rodents.

As 1665 rolled around, the bubonic plague had become a recurring nightmare that the people had grown accustomed to but did not understand. Scientists, scholars, and the greatest minds all tried to find a cure for the plague, only to find themselves defeated each time. The 14th century papal physician, Guy de Chauliac, put the shared sentiment into words: "The disease was most humiliating for the physicians, who were unable to render any assistance."

In England, the blame was blindly pinned onto an assortment of causes. Apart from divine intervention, the plague was believed to have been caused by certain planetary movements. Others claimed it had to do with the toxic fumes in the air. Then, there were those who theorized that their enemies had infiltrated their territory, poisoning the local wells to weaken its inhabitants. Some saw clues in the bad weather and their sick livestock, and found the abrupt explosion in the population of frogs, mice, flies, and other unwanted pests most suspicious.

Whatever the reason, the plague always loomed in the background, and in 1665, it would come back with a vengeance.

**A Familiar Chaos**

"We are all bound thither; we are hastening to the same common goal. Black death calls all things under the sway of its laws." – Ovid, Roman poet

One of the first signs that heralded the final wave of the third plague pandemic arose in December of 1664, not long after the seemingly portentous comet was sighted. The streets of London had only begun to simmer down when the grim tidings of the plague's return started to make its rounds. This red flag had been raised by a clergyman by the name of John Allen, who hailed from Amwell Street in London. One freezing night that winter, Allen popped into the Phillips residence for a visit. Allen was led up the creaking staircase and into the cluttered bedroom of the ill, a young, once fair maiden by the name of Mary, who had once been tried as a witch just a few years prior. The bedridden woman made no acknowledgment of the priest's presence, as she was much too preoccupied with writhing on the bed, her mind hopelessly lost in her restless, feverish state.

To Allen, these were the symptoms he had hoped he would never encounter again, but yet, here he was. Upon further inspection, an unmistakable boil the size of an apple was found protruding from the size of Mary's neck. He cringed as he watched the black and brown pus dribble out of the blistered bubo.

Allen stayed by Mary's side as her mother swept aside her scraggly, greasy hair, dabbing at the sweat trickling down her discolored face. The priest, who was certain the end was near, dutifully prayed with her for several hours, up until her last gasp of breath. Allen later wrote about the heartrending experience in a letter to his brother, lamenting, "In this fetid, grimy city, this poor soul departed this life in the greatest agony. She tossed and turned, this way and that, shouting for her deliverance. At 4 in the morn, the pestilence burst forth from the boils, destroying her at once."

Unbeknownst to the Londoners, the plague had made its stealthy return. A few at the time began to contemplate the "miasma" effect as a source of origin, suspecting the disease to be airborne. Apart from that conjecture, authorities were left baffled by the inexplicable terror that was the plague.

While Mary Phillips, along with a few other documented cases sprinkled around the city, were killed by the plague, the disease would not truly rear its head until a year later. Some today theorize its delay was brought about by the winter, and though these cases had ended in fatalities, the public had wishfully disregarded them as freak, one-off cases.

No one saw cause for alarm until the death of Rebecca Andrews. Rebecca was a resident of Cock and Key Alley, which belonged to the St. Dunstan's Parish by Fleet Street, one of the major streets in London. She lived amongst 30 other impoverished families of varying sizes, squeezed into a horridly crowded community with some of the foulest living conditions in the entire city. The local churchwarden, Henry Dorsett, oversaw the alley. The poor of Cock and Key held a special place in his heart, as he, too, had come from similar beginnings.

Rebecca, like her neighbors, was numb to the horrors of everyday life, and made do with what she had. She was fondly remembered for fostering orphans and disabled children running amok in the slums. At the time, she had taken in an abandoned boy named Laurence.

According to most sources, the date of Rebecca's death is listed as April 12, 1665. This was the same date another young woman by the name of Margaret Porteus succumbed to her infection. Porteous was later buried in Covent Garden, located south of St. Giles-in-the-Fields, just half a mile away from Cock and Key Alley.

Other sources, including the Channel 4 film documentary, *The Great Plague*, placed Rebecca's date of death on the 15th of June. The same film named Rebecca as patient zero of Cock and Key Alley, unknowingly signing the death warrants of the tiny community. A local physician had been sent over to her home, where he found her frail, barely-breathing body in the corner of the room. The instant the physician's eyes landed on the overt boil under her arm, the shade of his face matched her sickly primrose complexion. There was no denying it – Rebecca Andrews had the plague.

Authorities ordered for Rebecca's house to be sealed shut at once. She was quarantined alongside Laurence, who, upon the physician's first visit, had not yet displayed any symptoms of the disease. Still, a blacksmith was hired to attach a heavy padlock onto the front door. Planks of wood were nailed to all the doors and windows, leaving the widow and the orphan in a pitch-black vacuum of a prison. Neighbors took turns guarding the door to ensure that Laurence did not escape, as well as to prevent unapproved visits. About a week later, nurses returned and found Rebecca's limp body. Laurence might still have been blinking, but a boil had formed under his chin. Within the next 24 hours, the boy passed on, finally put out of his misery.

When signs of the plague began to crop up in various areas around London, people had no choice but to face the music. Another notable case was recounted in the diary of Samuel Pepys, an administrator in the English Navy and Member of Parliament. Pepys, most known for his religious journal writing, kept up his regular logging for over a decade. In his now celebrated and often referenced work, he recounted the savagery of the outbreak.

**Pepys**

On the 24th of July, the parish of Saint Olave Hart Street announced the death of Mary Ramsey, an indigent young girl who resided with her family in the spare room of a beggarly almshouse. This would be the first plague-related death recorded in this parish. The death of young Mary had come as a double-whammy for the Ramsey family, for her sister had been laid to rest just a day before, albeit from unrelated causes. A day after Mary Ramsey's death, another boy who shared a room with the Ramseys also died from the plague and was buried alongside them.

Accounts at the time asserted that it was Mary Ramsey who had brought the plague to London with her from France, where she was thought to have previously resided up to the early 1660s. Modern historians beg to differ; instead, they speculate that the disease had traveled all the way from the Netherlands. The Netherlands had always been a hub for the plague, so much so that its residents' leading causes of death had been marked by the disease since 1599. Dutch trading ships bearing cargoes of cotton from Amsterdam are said to have been the culprits, as the city had suffered an egregious outbreak between 1663 and 1664, losing up to 50,000 of its inhabitants. Upon realizing this, King Charles II of England canceled all trade with the Dutch in an effort to avert the disease's path, but by then, the king was powerless to stop it.

**King Charles II of England**

There remains considerable disagreement concerning the trigger to this vicious outbreak, mainly due to the inconsistency of the Bills of Mortality. These bills had been issued by Parliament in November of 1532, and were the equivalent of death certificates. Initially, these were strictly designed to keep track of the plague mortality rates in different parishes, and the practice of weekly transcriptions only began during the brief outbreak in London between December of 1592 and December of 1595.

The Bills of Mortality were retired fleetingly, but they were soon brought back during yet another outbreak in 1603. From then onward, it was used to record all the weekly deaths of each parish. An initial or symbol next to the name of deceased was added to these bills to indicate their cause of death. For the English parishes in the 1660s, these bills were inundated with name after name, almost all of which had the letter "P" next to them. As the outbreak persevered, these names were reduced to impersonal descriptions such as "boy," "girl," or "man in the street," as the bill writers could no longer keep abreast of the nonstop deaths.

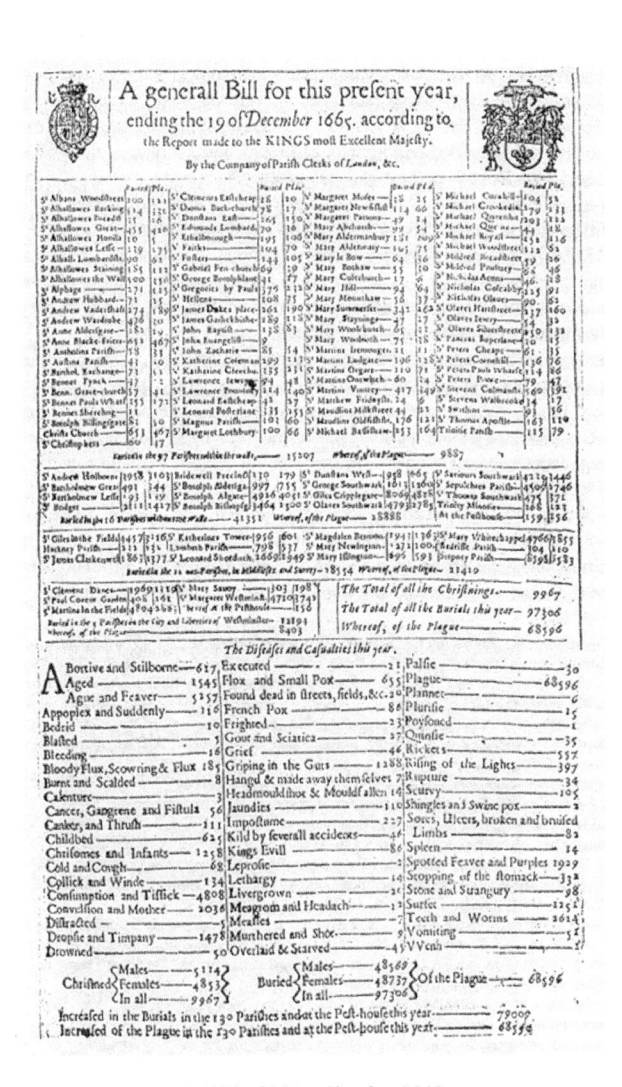

**A Bill of Mortality for 1665**

John Graunt, a well-to-do merchant with a passion for science and an honored member of the Fellowship of the Royal Academy, was one of the first to be entrusted with the record taking for these bills. As these bills were penned by different parishes and later compiled into one antiquated and heavily insecure database, certain missing dates, figures, and gaps in these logs remain unsolved. The irregularities of the record-keeping made it even trickier to properly identify the patient zeroes of any particular outbreak.

In July of 1665, the public of London found themselves backed into a corner, forced to stare the facts they had neglected – perhaps intentionally – to take seriously. The plague had returned in its full force. King Charles II and his entourage, foreseeing the threat, loaded up their carriages and made off for Salisbury, and later to Oxford.

Those who could afford it –wealthy merchants, lawyers, and other higher-ups in society – scooped up their families and left town. In October, Parliament also decided to make themselves scarce, rehousing in Oxford, where they joined the king. Packs of clergymen who elected to serve the community in spirit joined the refugees. Most of the doctors, including the College of Surgeons, declined to stay behind to look after the plague-stricken and instead hightailed it to the countryside.

All in all, an estimated 200,000 people deserted the city. Daniel Defoe, author of *Journal of the Plague Years*, explained the scene: "Nothing was to be seen but wagons and carts, with goods, women, servants, children, coaches, filled with people of the better sort, and horsemen attending them, all hurrying away."

**Defoe**

Among the braver souls who opted to forgo the disappearing act were a few dozen sheriffs, aldermen, and leaders of parishes. Perhaps most noteworthy of those who had stayed put was the Lord Mayor of London, Sir John Lawrence. Lawrence hoped to establish some sense of reassurance and order to what was left of the diminishing city. One of his first orders of business was the construction of a specially built booth, paneled with sturdy sheets of glass on all 4 sides. He spent all of his office hours sitting in this glass case. This way, he could serve the public and fend off the disease simultaneously.

Spearheaded by the Lord Mayor, the remaining authorities instituted a refined set of Plague Orders, colloquially referred to as the "Lord Mayor's Orders." These orders borrowed elements from past decrees such as Italy, a nation that has had more than plenty of experience with the plague. The orders were also upgraded with new regulations that satisfied the needs of the current situation. The compiled regulations were presented to the public on the 1st of July, but would only truly be enforced later that month.

To start with, Lawrence called for the aldermen to appoint at least 1-3 officials who were "of good sort and credit" to act as the "examiners" of each parish, a post that would be held for at least 2 months. Those who ditched their posts or refused to comply with duties assigned to them were imprisoned. Examiners were in charge of identifying and keeping tabs on infected households. They had the ability to order the provisional shut-in of suspicious households until the illness was officially diagnosed. If the ill displayed any symptoms, they were handed off to the constable to start the quarantine.

When a house had been rendered infected, a red cross was painted onto the doors of their homes, oftentimes, with the words "Lord have mercy upon us" scrawled on top of these symbols. Those who had come in contact with the diseased were required to wield dyed staffs at all times. More and more blacksmiths imposed themselves on infected homes, outfitting heavy-duty padlocks on their doors.

A pair of watchmen would also be posted outside the front doors of every infected household, working in alternating shifts around the clock. They would not only scope out potential intruders or absconders, they catered to all the food, drink, medical care, and other necessities of the sick. If the watchmen were to leave their post for any reason, they must double-check to ensure that the door has been bolted shut, and take the key with them. Those who failed to uphold their duties were either penalized or thrown behind bars. Likewise, unauthorized visitors who were discovered inside infected houses were forcefully locked in with the sick for a standard period of 40 days, with their release only permitted upon recovery. Needless to say, seeing daylight again was almost unheard of.

Women in the city were employed as "searchers." Searchers were the first to arrive on the scene and come in contact with the victims' corpses. They were a one-trick coroner of sorts, as their only job was to confirm the plague as the cause of death. Searchers often lodged together, but they were isolated from the rest of the public. Candidates were to be of "honest reputation," as these women vowed never to steal or take advantage of the deceased during their visits. Besides appointed physicians and nurses, the searchers were the only other people allowed in an infected household.

"Brokers of the dead" was a title given to those who visited these homes, scouring the place and corpse for money and other valuables. Profits derived from their sales were funneled back into the parish. The public funds were usually managed by the churchwarden or alderman, and its money used to purchase food, drink, and medication for the sick of the community.

In late July, the vacancy for grave diggers had doubled, as did the grisly specialty professions that nobody wanted. Under the mayor's orders, men from all over the city were rounded up and burdened with the slaughtering of 40,000 dogs and somewhere between 80,000 to 200,000 cats, to prevent the infection from spreading. Because these undesirable jobs required a strong stomach, they were compensated accordingly.

As the plague continued to spread, the mayor established a curfew for every parish. All taverns, inns, and other places of business or entertainment were to shut its doors by 9:00 p.m. every night. With time, the mayor's orders extended with more improved regulations. Gravediggers were to ensure that their graves were at least 6-feet deep, and all funerals and public gatherings prohibited.

The new regulations did not stop there. Fires were to be kept alight all 24 hours of the day, as it was believed to cleanse and purify the poisonous air. These fires were often scented with pepper and frankincense, which not only veiled the decay of the city but also acted as a disinfectant. Houses were ordered to be swept clean and scrubbed from top to bottom. The dumping of trash and waste outside homes and in the streets became punishable by law. Authorities also made sure to discipline those who broke into and out of the infected houses to steal from the infected and dead.

The awful morale at the time was unimaginable, but Lord Mayor Lawrence was applauded for his efficiency at keeping the public pantry fully stocked. London's remembrancer, who served as the medium of communication between the Lord Mayor and the public, praised his superior. He gushed, "Everything was managed with so much care and excellent order observed in the whole city, suburbs, that London may be a pattern and example to all cities of the world for the good government and excellent order that was everywhere kept even in the most violent infection and the people were in the utmost consternation and distress."

As driven as the mayor was, his critics deemed his laws overambitious, as they would prove difficult to enforce. Moreover, the deeper the plague penetrated, less were available to supervise all the infected houses at one time, and 18-20 watchmen were murdered at their posts. At times, the ill, driven to near madness from the forced and prolonged confinement, slipped a noose through the upper gap of the front door and lassoed it around the snoozing guard's neck, strangling him before breaking free.

What was more, even with all the measures set in place, as well as the admiration the mayor's determination had garnered from his peers, the number of plague-related deaths in London climbed. In the beginning of July, the death toll was at 267, but by the end of the month, that number had spiked to 2,020. Granted, Lawrence's supporters argued that the number would have been higher without the mayor's orders and safety tactics, but the morale was swiftly sinking all the same. It was an era of constant surveillance and vigilance.

Most of all, Londoners were clambering on top of one another to make it past the border, but they were hopelessly shackled. A month earlier, the mayor had barred the gates of the city shut. This was a controversial but necessary measure enacted to prevent London's infected residents from further spreading the disease to other cities. If one wanted to make it past that border, they would have to present a clean certificate of health. These certificates were commonly described as becoming "more valuable than gold." It was with this truth that a new side business was bred by forgers of the city, who produced counterfeit documents for those who could cough up the sum.

The mayor's worst fears had been realized. London's borders may have been closed, but the countless infected and counterfeit document holders who managed to escape spread the disease to nearby cities and towns anyway.

Around August of 1665, the plague had made its way to the village of Eyam in Derbyshire. Eyam was a small village that housed only 350 residents, headed by its parish and church leader, William Mompesson. That summer, a local tailor received a package of laundry from London. The tailor unwrapped the package and lurched back at once, retracting a hand crawling with ravenous fleas. He discarded the package, slapped at his hand repeatedly, and burnt the clothes as soon as he had a moment to spare, but the fleas had gotten the better of him. Within a week, the tailor was dead, found with an ugly boil peeking out from behind his collar.

By the end of September, 5 more in Eyam had died from the plague. In the next month, that number was raised to 23. As the deaths continued to escalate, the frightened villagers begged Mompesson for permission to flee to the plague-free Sheffield in northern England. With a heavy heart, Mompesson attempted to and succeeded in coaxing his villagers into staying so that the disease could be contained. Mompesson continued to preach, but his services were relocated outside of town to minimize the chance of infection to the flock, many of whom had come from nearby cities. Neighboring communities who learned of their heroism came to their aid. Food was left on the parish stones by the border of Eyam. Coins were also dropped into jars of vinegar next to these stones.

Eventually, up to 260 of Eyam's 350 inhabitants would waste away from the disease. Among the dead was Mompesson's wife. As for the preacher, he lived to see the plague run its course.

**Therapy**

"To the Exchange, where I have not been in a great while. But, 'Lord!' how sad a sight is to see streets empty of people. Jealous of every door that one sees shut... God preserve us all." – Samuel Pepys

Those who were left behind to defend themselves began to set up their own precautions. Almost every single inhabitant that had been abandoned in London was well below the poverty line, and their distress, along with the plague, was understandably thriving. After all, these people, as one historian put it, were the "human fuel for an epidemic."

The remaining Londoners worked to uphold the best sanitary standards their environment allowed them. Businessmen and merchants, like those who came to the aid of the villagers at Eyam, deposited coins into vinegar jars as a means of sterilization. Raw meat at butcher shops was no longer handled by hand but instead with hooks. Letters received from within or outside the city walls were intercepted by authorities, and all sealed documents were waved over the smoke arising from cauldrons of boiling vinegar before they were opened.

People taught their children to inspect themselves every night before bed, on the constant lookout for any buboes of visible symptoms. Apart from the bubo, which averaged about the size of a chicken egg, they searched for dark discoloration and swelling around the neck. More signs that alluded to any of the 3 strains of plague included fevers, chills, nausea, headaches, sudden fatigues, abdominal pain, diarrhea, vomiting, irregular bleeding, and gangrene in the nose, toes, or fingers.

Those who were responsible for caring for the diseased also took unique precautions of their own. One such example was the costume most plague physicians and nurses wore during the visits to the infected patients' homes. Since most believed and promoted the miasma theory, those giving care wore distinctive metal masks fitted with a long beak, the creation of a French doctor named Charles de Lorme in 1619. The beaks were packed with an aromatic blend of spices, herbs, and dried flowers to combat the foul odors, as well as the toxicity in the air. These masks, now often associated with the plague, were often paired with a waxen coat that covered one from head to toe for whole-body protection, completing the "beak doctor costume."

The absent physicians who sought refuge in the countryside began to roll out one publication after another containing cures and safeguards for the people back home, and as the outbreak intensified, more scholars and enterprising minds stepped forward with "educated" suggestions of their own. Among these publications was one assembled by the Royal College of Physicians, *For the Cure of the Plague, As for the Preventing of Infection.*

The wordily-titled guidebook, which presented precautions and advice on how to fumigate houses and articles of clothing, as well as natural scent-related remedies, concluded with a section of recipes. These recipes were split in 2 parts, one devoted to rich, and one for the poor.

Many of the well-received remedies for the "richer sort" involved the use of powdered unicorn horn and crushed emeralds. These false remedies, often advertised as "plague water," were a common scam employed by crooks of the time that pounced on the chance to swindle the frantic and weak-minded. Another recipe instructed the rich to ingest 3 grams of Laudanum a day; this opiate powder was to be stirred into brandy for good measure. The poor were offered solutions that cost little to nothing, such as arsenic amulets that could be worn around the neck or clamped under one's arms. 10-year-old treacle was taken as a plague-rejecting vitamin.

Recipes for pastes were also provided for women or children who preferred to avoid bitter-tasting remedies. One of these concoctions involved the grinding and mixing of rose petals, wood sorrel, sage flowers, wood syrup, harts-horn shavings, and more, which was to be coated on twice a day. Other recipes pertained to perfumes or portable scented satchels. One formula called for wormwood, myrrh, valerian, snake-root, and a variety of other hard-to-find herbs and roots.

As a method of pain relief, the rich often turned to fine wine and other agents to curb the intolerable agony. The poor turned to smoking tobacco, which at the time was commended for its healing and allegedly disease-deterring properties. Samuel Pepys was one of those who publicly advocated for this method, and he was known for chewing tobacco to keep himself free of the disease.

Children were no exception. In fact, they were encouraged to partake in these cures, and if they had the gall to refuse the pipe, they would often be beaten or disciplined by their guardians. As discussed in the account of a scholar from Eton, the year the plague reached its peak, all the boys in school were ordered to puff on a tobacco pipe every morning. Those that disobeyed were flogged. Children were also prescribed medicinal drinks that contained severe levels of alcohol and opium.

The surviving apothecaries of London were often sold out of the most bizarre cures and prophylactics, which also impacted the market. For instance, rosemary, a favored stench-masker, was previously priced at a shilling for a large sack. During the plague, that price jumped as high as 6 shillings for a meager handful.

The use of lucky charms was another doctor-endorsed measure. Dr. George Thomson, for one, was remembered for wearing a dead toad as a necklace. Another eccentric charm was a scroll of parchment tucked into the clothes of Londoners featuring the words "abracadabra," its letters written in triangular form. Others, following doctors' recommendations, sported a rabbit's foot or covered themselves with leeches.

Buboes were lanced and drained, and while it has now been concluded to be harmful and ineffective, it was seen as one of the only practical cures and pain relief techniques of the time. Fully-plucked chickens were then strapped onto the bubo or open sore, as people believed this transferred all the bacteria to the clucking and squirming animal. Another particularly dangerous cure was the consuming of arsenic and mercury syrups.

The church also chimed in, promoting a cure of their own – the power of prayer.

**The Peak**

"The sad news of the death of so many in the parish of the plague, 40 last night, the bell always going... either for deaths or burials." – Samuel Pepys

By August of 1665, the Bills of Mortality indicated that up to 7,000 victims a week were tagged with the plague as their cause of death. As a grave reminder, these were statistics that purely pertained to Christian parishes; the Jews, Quakers, Muslims, and other non-Christians across England went uncounted.

The facilities in London that were constructed to counter the plague were grossly insufficient when it came to serving the speedily rising numbers of the sick public. During the mass exodus of London's wealthy class, a nobleman and soldier, William, 1st Earl of Craven, chose to stay behind. Along with the Lord Mayor's orders, William called for the establishment of more pest houses, otherwise referred to as "plague houses," as well as the bulk burial of the deceased in enormous plague pits. As the plague continued to slither across the city, he hastily ordered the purchases of unused land, and transformed buildings into pest houses in Lancaster Gate, as well as the parishes of St. Clement Danes, St. Paul, St. James, and St. Martin-in-the-Fields. And yet, these pest houses could do nothing to dampen the fury of the plague.

Records from these pest houses have been clumsily misplaced by the hands of time. Therefore, modern experts have found it problematic to determine the extent of the effectiveness when it comes to these makeshift plague hospitals. Today, there are some who agree that the isolation of the sick in these establishments, albeit suffering extraordinarily substandard sanitary conditions, helped reduce the number of victims to a certain degree. On the other hand, there are those who argue that the rise in these forced quarantines and confinements in grungy and cramped spaces only helped to perpetuate the disease, and as such, was responsible for the lengthening of the Bills of Mortality. One scholar observed, "Infection may have killed its thousands, but shutting up have killed its ten-thousands."

Moreover, as these pest houses were privately owned and unregulated by the government, they earned a nasty reputation of their own. The condemnation of these pest houses repelled many from venturing through its front doors. Since the majority of doctors and trained physicians were nowhere to be found, most of the pest houses were staffed with only nurses, many of them vastly inexperienced. These nurses were also often uneducated and hired straight off the streets, no qualifications needed.

Perhaps unsurprisingly, despite the fact that these nurses had accepted a job no one dared touch with a 10-foot pole, the public's anger was often projected to these nurses, who were accused of further spreading the disease. The nurses soon found themselves surrounded by reputation-destructing hearsay, often unfounded. They were accused of scheming to murder their patients for ill-gotten gains. These "wretches," as many grew to call them, were supposedly strangling and suffocating their patients behind closed doors. Once the victim ceased their struggling, the nurses swooped in like gold-digging vultures and picked the corpse clean. Their greed was demonstrated through their recklessness in caring for the sick but unsettling shrewdness when it came to plundering their defenseless victims. Other nurses were accused of extracting "pestilential taint" from the bleeding sores of the sick. The goo was then allegedly bottled up, later to be secretly injected into the healthy, as a mode of shady but stable income. Regardless of the popularity of these warped narratives, records from Cock and Key Alley presented proof of a certain Nurse Fletcher that contradicted that stereotype. After stumbling upon valuables that amounted to more than a month's salary in one of the victim's homes, she reportedly returned every last shilling to the parish that same day.

Meanwhile, the restlessness among the trapped Londoners soared. Many vocally protested the policy of imprisoning all the occupants of an infected household, and they fought to find a way for uninfected occupants to flee before the clock ran out. Watchmen standing guard outside quarantined homes, along with guards by the city border, were often bribed by those seeking to escape, while others paid off officials to overlook plague symptoms in their homes. Some families were so hell-bent on fleeing that they left all their belongings and deserted their homes, choosing to live with nothing on the streets rather than risk permanent house arrest.

Those who were locked up in quarantine had to conjure up escape methods that required much more creativity. Other than the last-resort "fishing for guards" technique, which involved the use of a noose, some armed themselves with spoons, shovels, and other tools in an effort to tunnel their way out to freedom. Others attempted adrenaline-fueled rooftop escapes. There were also those who persuaded their friends to slip poison or sleep-inducing drugs into the watchmen's food to clear the coast.

Those at their wits' end set fire to their homes. A few hacked away at the weakest walls in their abodes but were almost always immediately tackled to the ground by the watchmen. In one incredible episode, a man attached a contraption made out of fireworks to his door and detonated the bomb, leaping out with his family through the window in the nick of time.

On the 12th of August, the Lord Mayor, who could no longer ignore the unremittingly plummeting morale, made a decisive attempt to bring back a sense of unity. For one night only, the healthy were ordered inside their homes by 9:00 p.m. to allow those that had been locked up outside of their homes for a few hours. The momentarily freed captives were swathed in thick cloths and scarves from head to toe so that they could experience the ephemeral "liberty of [going] abroad for air." That night, the physically fit peered out of their windows, watching as a mob of the zombie-like plague patients roamed the streets. While stepping outside would have meant joining the condemned, many were tempted to burst out of their homes and into the crowd, as some would have spotted loved ones they had not seen for close to a month. Even more heartbreaking, the faces detected were most likely those they would never see again.

By September of 1665, London's plague-related mortality rates saw yet another unwanted spike. Now, between 8,000-10,000 Londoners were dying each week. Gradually, circumstances devolved into such a sorry state that most municipal authorities had given up on enforcing the preventative measures they had worked so hard to promote. What was left of the watchmen no longer stood guard outside quarantined homes. Their duties were instead redirected to the handling of the dead.

*Plague in 1665.*

**A depiction of corpses being buried in London in 1665**

Communal burial pits became an equally chilling reality of the plague. These plague pits only multiplied, as bodies racked up faster than personal graves could be dug. The sight of "plague carts" driving up and down the streets of London became routine. The drivers of these harrowing death vehicles were often heard crying out to the public, "Bring out your dead!"

At first, authorities worried that the number of bodies would add to the alarm of an already disconcerted public, so the Lord Mayor ordered for all plague pit burials to be scheduled after curfew hours. This policy was altered not long after when authorities realized that doing so had cut the precious burial time in half. This would not do, as this meant that the stacks of decomposing bodies, including those of children, in infected households, streets, and alleys, which were quickly piling up, would be left unattended. Once again, drivers of plague carts resumed their daytime duties.

During the outbreak's worst phases, these drivers dumped entire carts of bodies into these pits, all at once, to save time. The Aldgate parish featured one of the largest plague pits, stretching 50-feet long and 20-feet wide, said to fit over 1,100 corpses. Other plague sites around London included the parishes of St. Bride's, Finsbury Fields, Goswell Street, Golden Square in Soho, and several in the St. Dunstan area.

Those who dreamt of fleeing saw their wills strained until their conviction ultimately fizzled out. The church bells that signaled the death of a victim rang for hours on end, until the mere act of tolling the bell no longer made sense. Continuing to do so would have required a new man for the post, a full-time commitment at that.

At this stage of the outbreak, those who were left were hollow shells of their past selves. To put matters in perspective, the loved ones who had dropped dead around the average Londoner either amounted to or surpassed the number and heartache that would have been otherwise distributed over a lifetime. More than ever, it became easier for them to latch onto theories that might have seemed downright ludicrous in a different setting.

A dubious theory from Paris soon crossed London's borders. Word began to spread that diseases such as pox or syphilis, the latter a highly contagious sexually transmitted disease, could make one immune to the plague. This rumor prompted the healthy to frequent brothels for easy access to the STD. Some of the infected paid for sex with prostitutes in the hopes of replacing one poison with a lesser disease that came with a better chance of survival. Another myth supported by dicey medieval science asserted that diseases, including the plague, could be erased through intercourse with a virgin of either gender. Consequently, this resulted in an increase in underage victims.

Towards the end of 1665, the Bills of Mortality published a total of 68,594 plague deaths in its

London registry. Experts believe that these figures have also been seriously distorted over the years because the leading causes of death that followed were suspected to have been associated with the plague. Among the other leading causes were 4,664 who died of "fever," 3,173 to "consumption," (a retired term for tuberculosis),1,855 to "spotted fever," (also known as meningitis or typhus), and finally, 1,931 to "teething," which referred to toddlers who died during or before the completion of their teething stage.

### A Storm Weathered and a Winter's Thaw

"'Should evil come upon us, the sword, or judgment, or pestilence, or famine, we will stand before this house and before You (for your name is in this house) and cry to You in our distress, and You will hear and deliver us.'" – 2 Chronicles 20:9

Even with the patent fire hazards that came with the fumigation process, the trend began to catch on. Fumigation was championed by the officials of London, a practice proposed by one James Angier. Back in June, Angier had managed to persuade the Privy Council into allowing him to conduct an experiment of his own to test out the process. The trials transpired in a ramshackle house in Newton Street, close to Holborn. Of the 12 occupants in the residence, 4 had already expired from the plague, while 2 of the remaining 8 showed hints of the disease.

The fumigation process entailed the burning of a medley of saltpeter (another term for potassium nitrate), amber, and brimstone. The stupendous stench caused by the burning of these materials was said to have been so profound that it drove off all the rodents, fleas, and pests from a household. As the experiment concluded, there were no more recorded deaths in the post-fumigated home.

When King Charles II learned of the vigorous acclamation surrounding Angier's pioneering germicide techniques, he demanded for all the structures within London to undergo this treatment. Tremendous shipments of coal were purchased for the daunting task. The coal would be used to kindle giant, crackling fires that would serve as fumigants for every 6 houses. As the clouds of smoke, steeped in the fragrance of sweet herbs, swirled over the city, Londoners were filled with renewed hope. It seemed as if the city of London could be saved, after all.

Regrettably, this sense of hope soon tapered off when the weather experienced a sudden mood swing. The thundering skies turned gray, its tears dousing the flames across the city. When the skies eventually cleared, the citizens of London dragged themselves out of their shelters and went to work on resuscitating the flames.

Slowly but surely, it appeared as if the winter of 1665 had once again erected a roadblock against the disease. As the Bills of Mortality continued to shrink, those who had decamped began their cautious trek back home. Some of those who had returned, perhaps in some way racked with the guilt of their departure, began to look after the ill.

Sadly, the immune systems of a large number of these returning refugees failed to combat the ghastly plague, making them highly susceptible to the disease. They soon fell victim to their newly contracted infections, contributing to the brief rise in the death toll in December of 1665. Luckily for London, this proved to be no more than a deceptive glint in the pan, and in the weeks that followed, the plague began to wane. The intervals between Bills of Mortality updates grew longer and longer.

When February of 1666 rolled around, the outbreak was officially declared dormant. That same month, the king and his family, along with the justices, court officials, and members of Parliament, returned to the city. While Parliament had returned, the governing body would not be formally reinstated until September that year. By the following month's end, Edward Hyde, the Lord Chancellor and 1st Earl of Clanderon, summarized the resolution of the revived city in a letter, writing that "the streets were as full, the exchange as much crowded, and the people, in all places as numerous, as they had ever been, few persons missing any of their acquaintance…"

Under the command of Parliament's Rebuilding of London Act 1666, business picked up where it had left off. Trade resumed. The boards to quarantined homes were prised off, the structures dismantled, and rebuilt. Shops and places of entertainment reopened their doors. The cragged and damaged roads in the central areas of London were stripped and repaved with smoother and wider streets. New sewage systems were developed to help boost the city's sanitation standards. This was a project that would take over a decade to complete, headed by Robert Hooke, the Surveyor of London.

In May of that year, the Privy Council of the city reinstituted a revised version of the plague orders, prohibiting the burial of future plague-stricken corpses in churchyards. The council also required its residents to use quicklime – cement or mortar produced by heating limestone – in approved burial sites. None of these graves were to be disturbed for a minimum of 1 year, as this helped to ensure that the disease could no longer be contracted by anyone coming into contact with these corpses.

The outbreak might have been declared obsolete, but in the months that followed, a few cases of plague-related deaths popped up intermittently across the nation. These periodic cases would appear in the mid-summer of 1666, up until the last-ever outbreak-related case in 1669.

As 1666 carried on, it seemed as if things could only go better from there, but Londoners were sorely mistaken. On the 2nd of September, a fire erupted in King's Bakery in Pudding Lane, close to the fabled London Bridge. Fires were a relatively common occurrence during the time, but the "tinder-dry" and uncharacteristically rain-less heat allowed the fire to proliferate almost effortlessly. An estimated 300 structures were said to have been burned to the ground before the fire was finally extinguished 4 days later. Still and all, there were those that saw a silver lining in the catastrophe; some came to believe that the disastrous fire had been the key to stamping out the plague in London once and for all. Today, modern historians believe that the plague had already tapered off before the disaster, and by the time it was gone, an estimated 100,000 Londoners had died in less than 16 months.

Theories aimed at determining what caused the end of the outbreaks that claimed over 200 million people by the end of its run continue to surface to this day. Some say it was the fumigation, quarantine, and other preventative measures that did away with the plague. Others contend that it had been the consistent improvements in personal hygiene in the years that followed. A definitive theory has yet to be found. How the "super survivors" of the plague, particularly those that never left London, could have built such an immunity, is another mystery that has yet to be solved.

In recent years, new findings have come forth concerning the cause of the plague itself, leading to some historians backtracking on previous prevailing theories. Back in 2001, scholars from Liverpool University suggested that the plague might have been caused by a virus much like Ebola, as opposed to the *yersinia pestis* bacterium. That same year, historian Norman Cantor proposed that the plague had been the result of anthrax, citing the anthrax spores found in Scotland during the time.

In 2015, scientists around the world fought to refute the theory that the plague had been manufactured by rats. For a time, gerbils were put on the hot seat, but that hypothesis was quickly put to rest. In September of the next year, tests from Germany confirmed the presence of the *yersinia pestis* bacterium from samples that had been found at an excavation site in Liverpool Street.

The horrors of the plague may seem like nothing more than a foul and fickle fiend of yesteryear, but this is a foe that can never be fully vanquished. Even now, an average of 7 plague cases are still reported each year in the United States alone.

## The Great Fire

Chapter 1: A Sad and Lamentable Accident

An advertisement for a fire engine on wheels that boasts, "These Engins, (which are the best) to quinch great Fires; are made by John Keeling in Black Fryers (after many years' Experience)."

A model of Keeling's fire engines

"The ordinary course of this paper having been interrupted by a sad and lamentable accident of Fire lately happened in the City of London: It hath been thought fit for satisfying the minds of so many of his Majesties good subjects who must needs be concerned for the Issue of so great an accident, to give this short, but true Account of it." - Excerpt from an article published in the *London Gazette* on September 11, 1666.

Unlike many natural and manmade disasters, everyone in London learned pretty quickly how the Great Fire started. The city had been plagued by a remarkable drought for nearly a year when, just as September 1st became September $2^{nd}$, Thomas Farriner's banked fire sent sparks out onto the floor of his bakery. He and his family, living above the shop, were awakened by the smell of smoke and crawled through their own windows to those of the house next door, where they escaped. Their family maid was not as fortunate as her employers and perished when panic gripped her and left her too scared to attempt to make it to the other house.

At first, it seemed that Farriner and his neighbors might be able to put out the fire themselves, but after trying for an hour to beat out the blaze, they decided to contact the authorities, who in turn ordered that the houses on either side of the two now burning should be destroyed to create a firebreak. While London had firefighters that formed units known as "Trained Bands" and people who patrolled the streets to be on the lookout for just such an incident, it was common to pull down houses in an effort to stop a fire from growing out of control, to the extent that churches were required to store "firehooks" used to pull down buildings and create firebreaks.

**A 17th century illustration depicting the use of firehooks alongside more traditional methods of fighting fire**

Naturally, those who owned these homes were not fond of that idea, so they appealed to Sir Thomas Bloodworth, then Lord Mayor of London, to save their homes. By the time he arrived and assessed the situation, more homes were ablaze and the city's firefighters begged him to let them tear down the nearest houses. A quintessential politician, he refused to create a firebreak for fear of angering the absentee landlords who rented out some of the houses. Instead, he downplayed the danger and allegedly said of the burgeoning fire, "Pish! A woman could piss it out!" With that, he returned home to go to bed, a fateful decision decried by many in the days after the blaze, including Samuel Pepys, a young politician who kept one of England's most famous diaries. Just a few days after the fire was finished, Pepys complained in his diary, "People do all the world over cry out of the simplicity [stupidity] of my Lord Mayor in general; and more particularly in this business of the fire, laying it all upon him."

**Pepys**

Indeed, Bloodworth could not have been more wrong about the severity of the fire, and by 3:00 a.m. on Sunday, September 2, the fire could be seen across the city. Samuel Pepys described the scene in his diary: "Some of our maids sitting up late last night to get things ready against our feast to-day, Jane called us up about three in the morning, to tell us of a great fire they saw in the City. So I rose, and slipped on my night-gown, and went to her window; and thought it to be on the back-side of Marke-lane at the farthest, but being unused to such fires as followed, I thought it far enough off; and so went to bed again, and to sleep."

Since Pepys was himself an official in the English government, when he saw that the fire was still burning in the morning, he decided to investigate the situation for himself: "About seven rose again to dress myself, and there looked out at the window, and saw the fire not so much as it was, and further off. So to my closet to set things to rights, after yesterday's cleaning. By and by Jane comes and tells me that she hears that above 300 houses have been burned down to-night by the fire we saw, and that it is now burning down all Fish-street, by London Bridge. So I made myself ready presently, and walked to the Tower, and there got up upon one of the high places, Sir J. Robinson's little son going up with me; and there I did see the houses at that end of the bridge all on fire, and an infinite great fire on this and the other side the end of the bridge; which, among other people, did trouble me for poor little Michell and our Sarah on the bridge. So down with my heart full of trouble to the Lieutenant of the Tower, who tells me that it begun this morning in the King's baker's [His name was Faryner] house in Pudding-lane, and that it hath burned down St. Magnes Church and most part of Fish-street already."

Concerned about what he was seeing, Pepys used his authority with the Royal Navy to commandeer a boat and sail down the Thames to get a better look at what was going on. He recorded in his diary, "So I [went] down to the water-side, and there got a boat, and through bridge, and there saw a lamentable fire. Poor Michell's house, as far as the Old Swan, already burned that way, and the fire running further, that in a very little time it got as far as the Steele-yard, while I was there. Everybody endeavoring to remove their goods, and flinging into the river, or bringing them into lighters that lay off; poor people staying in their houses as long as till the very fire touched them, and then running into boats, or clambering from one pair of stairs by the water-side to another. And among other things, the poor pigeons, I perceive, were loath to leave their houses, but hovered about the windows and balconies, till they burned their wings, and fell down."

The more he saw, the more Pepys realized something needed to be done to stop the fire from spreading any further, but he did not see anyone making a concerted effort to actually put out the blaze. This was no doubt due in large measure to the size of the blaze, which compelled people to attempt to escape from the fire, not fight it. In fact, the fire was already so out of control that it was creating its own windstorm as it sucked in more and more air to feed its ravaging appetite. Pepys witnessed this and wrote, "Having staid, and in an hour's time seen the fire rage every way, and nobody, to my sight, endeavoring to quench it, but to remove their goods, and leave all to the fire, and having seen it get as far as the Steele-yard, and the wind mighty high, and driving it into the City: and everything after so long a drought proving combustible, even the very stones of churches, and among other things, the poor steeple [of St. Lawrence Poultney] by which pretty Mrs. (?) lives, and whereof my old schoolfellow Elborough is parson, taken fire in the very top, and there burned till it fell down; I to White Hall (with a gentleman with me, who desired to go off from the Tower, to see the fire, in my boat): and there up to the King's closet in the Chapel, where people come about me, and I did give them an account dismayed them all, and word was carried in to the King. So I was called for, and did tell the King and Duke of York what I saw, and that unless his Majesty did command houses to be pulled down, nothing could stop the fire."

**The Duke of York**

**Chapter 2: A Violent Easterly Wind Fomented It**

"On the second instant, at one of the clock in the Morning, there happened to break out, a sad and deplorable Fire in Pudding-lane, near New Fish-street, which falling out at that hour of the night, and in a quarter of the Town so close built with wooden pitched houses spread itself so far before the day, and with such distraction to the inhabitants and Neighbors, that care was not taken for the timely preventing the further diffusion of it, by pulling down houses, as ought to have been; so that this lamentable Fire in a short time became too big to be mastered by any Engines or working near it. It fell out most unhappily too, that a violent Easterly wind fomented it, and kept it burning all that day, and the night following spreading itself up to Grace-church-street and downwards from Cannon-street to the Water-side, as far as the Three Cranes in the Vintry." - Excerpt from an article published in the *London Gazette* on September 11, 1666.

In 1666, England's king was Charles II, who was widely respected for demonstrating an interest in taking care of his subjects. He had been returned to the throne following England's bloody civil wars and was a popular alternative to the Puritan government that had been headed by Oliver Cromwell a few years earlier. Pepys mentioned his meeting with the king during the emergency: "They seemed much troubled, and the King commanded me to go to my Lord Mayor from him, and command him to spare no houses, but to pull down before the fire every way. The Duke of York bid me tell him, that if he would have any more soldiers, he shall: and so did my Lord Arlington afterwards, as a great secret. Here meeting with Captain Cocke, I in his coach, which he lent me, and Creed with me to Paul's, and there walked along Watling-street, as well as I could, every creature coming away loaded with goods to save, and here and there sick people carried away in beds. Extraordinary good goods carried in carts-and on backs. At last met my Lord Mayor in Canning-street, like a man spent, with a handkerchief about his neck. To the King's message, he cried, like a fainting woman, 'Lord! what can I do? I am spent: people will not obey me. I have been pulling down houses; but the fire overtakes us faster than we can do it.' That he needed no more soldiers; and that, for himself, he must go and refresh himself, having been up all night."

**King Charles II**

Needless to say, Pepys was not impressed with Bloodworth's response to the crisis and decided to continue to take matters into his own hands. By this time, he was also concerned about his own home and family: "So he left me, and I him, and walked home; seeing people all almost distracted, and no manner of means used to quench the fire. The houses too so very thick thereabouts, and full of matter for burning, as pitch and tar, in Thames-street; and warehouses of oil, and wines, and brandy, and other things. Here I saw Mr. Isaac Houblon, the handsome man, prettily dressed and dirty at his door at Dowgate, receiving some of his brother's things, whose houses were on fire; and, as he says, have been removed twice already; and he doubts (as it soon proved) that they must be in a little time removed from his house also, which was a sad consideration. And to see the churches all filling with goods by people, who themselves should have been quietly there at this time. By this time it was about twelve o'clock; and so home, and there find my guests, who were Mr. Wood and his wife Barbary Shelden, and also Mr. Moone; she mighty fine, and her husband, for aught I see, a likely man. But Mr. Moone's design and mine, which was to look over my closet, and please him with the sight thereof, which he hath long desired, was wholly disappointed; for we were in great trouble and disturbance at this fire, not knowing what to think of it."

Of course, many others across the city were also concerned about how the fire was spreading. John Evelyn, a member of the king's court, wrote in his own diary: "I had public prayers at home. After dinner the fire continuing, with my Wife and Son took Coach and went to the bank side in Southwark, where we beheld that dismal spectacle, the whole City in dreadful flames near the Water side, and had now consumed all the houses from the bridge all Thames Street and upwards towards Cheape side, down to the three Cranes, and so returned exceedingly astonished, what would become of the rest."

**John Evelyn**

Meanwhile, Pepys still had his family and guests to think about, and since his own home was not in any imminent danger, he decided to continue on with his evening as originally planned. He later admitted, "[W]e had an extraordinary good dinner, and as merry as at this time we could be. While at dinner Mrs. Batelier come to enquire after Mr. Woolf and Stanes, (who it seems are related to them,) whose houses in Fish-street are all burned, and they in a sad condition. She would not stay in the fright. Soon as dined, I and Moone away, and walked through the City, the streets full of nothing but people, and horses and carts loaded with goods, ready to run over one another, and removing goods from one burned house to another. They now removing out of Canning-street (which received goods in the morning) into Lumbard-street, and further: and among others I now saw my little goldsmith Stokes receiving some friend's goods, whose house itself was burned the day after."

Having seen his guests safely home, Pepys decided to return to the river and see if there was anything else that he could do to help those in peril. He explained, "We parted at Paul's; he home, and I to Paul's Wharf, where I had appointed a boat to attend me, and took in Mr. Carcasse and his brother, whom I met in the street, and carried them below and above bridge too. And again to see the fire, which was now got further, both below and above, and no likelihood of stopping it. Met with the King and Duke of York in their barge, and with them to Queenhith, and there called Sir Richard Brown to them. Their order was only to pull down houses apace, and so below bridge at the water-side; but little was or could be done, the fire coming upon them so fast. Good hopes there was of stopping it at the Three Cranes above, and at Buttolph's Wharf below bridge, if care be used; but the wind carries it into the City, so as we know not by the water-side what it do there. River full of lighters and boats taking in goods, and good goods swimming in the water, and only I observed that hardly one lighter or boat in three that had the goods of a house in, but there was a pair of Virginalls [a musical instrument similar to a piano]."

Of course, Pepys was not the only person hoping to see the fire. Although those directly in its path were busy fleeing, there were many officials in charge of the situation, and there were also plenty of curious citizens who were turning out to see the blaze and the chaos that it was causing. According to Pepys, "Having seen as much as I could now, I away to White Hall by appointment, and there walked to St. James's Park, and there met my wife and Creed and Wood and his wife, and walked to my boat; and there upon the water again, and to the fire up and down, it still increasing, and the wind great. So near the fire as we could for smoke; and all over the Thames, with one's faces in the wind, you were almost burned with a shower of fire-drops. This is very true: so as houses were burned by these drops and flakes of fire, three or four, nay, five or six houses, one from another. When we could endure no more upon the water, we to a little ale-house on the Bankside, over against the Three Cranes, and there staid till it was dark almost, and saw the fire grow, and as it grew darker, appeared more and more, and in corners and upon steeples, and between churches and houses, as far as we could see up the hill of the City, in a most horrid malicious bloody flame, not like the fine flame of an ordinary fire. Barbary and her husband away before us."

## Chapter 3: Down the Hill to the Bridge

"The people in all parts about it, distracted by the vastness of it, and their care to carry away their Goods, many attempts were made to stop the spreading of it by pulling down Houses, and making great Intervals, but all in vain, the Fire seizing upon the Timber and Rubbish, and so continuing it set even through those spaces, and raging in a bright flame all Monday and Tuesday, notwithstanding His Majesties own, and His Royal Highness's indefatigable and personal pains to apply all possible remedies to prevent it, calling upon and helping the people with their Guards; and a great number of Nobility and Gentry unwearily assisting therein, for which they were requited with a thousand blessings from the poor distressed people." - Excerpt from an article published in the London Gazette on September 11, 1666

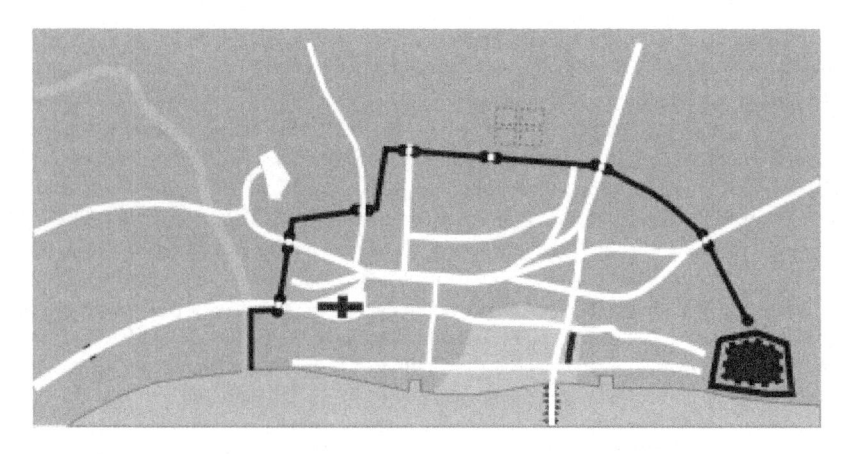

**The spread of the fire by Sunday evening, September 2**

As night fell on Sunday evening, all hopes of putting the fire out anytime soon vanished, so Pepys and others far enough away to still be out of danger returned home to pray for rain and a decent night's sleep. Alas, most would have neither, as Pepys noted in his diary: "We staid till, it being darkish, we saw the fire as only one entire arch of fire from this to the other side the bridge, and in a bow up the hill for an arch of above a mile long: it made me weep to see it. The churches, houses, and all on fire, and flaming at once; and a horrid noise the flames made, and the cracking houses at their ruin. So home with a sad heart, and there find everybody discoursing and lamenting the fire; and poor Tom Hater come with some few of his goods saved out of his house, which was burned upon Fish-street Hill. I invited him to lie at my house, and did receive his goods, but was deceived in his lying there, the news coming every moment of the growth of the fire; so as we were forced to begin to pack up our own goods, and prepare for their removal; and did by moonshine (it being brave dry and moonshine and warm weather) carry much of my goods into the garden, and Mr. Hater and I did remove my money and iron chests into my cellar, as thinking that the safest place. And got my bags of gold into my office, ready to carry away, and my chief papers of accounts also there, and my tallies into a box by themselves. So great was our fear, as Sir W. Batten hath carts come out of the country to fetch away his goods this night. We did put Mr. Hater, poor man, to bed a little; but he got but very little rest, so much noise being in my house, taking down of goods."

As the sun rose on Monday morning, September 3, those living to the northwest of the fire's original location were becoming increasingly concerned. John Evelyn noted in his diary, "The Fire having continued all this night (if I may call that night, which was as light as day for 10 miles round about after a dreadful manner) when conspiring with a fierce Eastern Wind, in a very dry season, I went on foot to the same place, when I saw the whole South part of the City burning from Cheape side to the Thames, and all along Cornehill (for it likewise kindled back against the Wind, as well [as] forward) Tower-Streete, Fen-church-street, Gracious Streete, and so along to Bainard Castle, and was now taking hold of St. Pauls-Church, to which the Scaffalds contributed exceedingly. The Conflagration was so universal, and the people so astonished, that from the beginning (I know not by what desponding or fate), they hardly stirred to quench it, so as there was nothing heard or seen but crying out and lamentation, and running about like distracted creatures, without at all attempting to save even their goods; such a strange consternation there was upon them, so as it burned both in breadth and length, The Churches, Public Halls, Exchange, Hospitals, Monuments, and ornaments, leaping after a prodigious manner from house to house and street to street, at great distance one from the other, for the heat (with a long set of faire and warm weather) had even ignited the air, and prepared the materials to conceive the fire, which devoured after a[n] incredible manner, houses, furniture, and everything.

On September 3, even the famous London Bridge was in danger, though in the end it did not burn. However, the fire was most certainly heading for the banks that held most of the city's treasure, and as a result, depositors were often forced to choose between their homes and possessions and their gold, investments on which the wealthiest in town depended. Most of the gold was rescued, but the Royal Exchange, a 17th century version of a shopping mall, was lost. Pepys recorded in his diary, "About four o'clock in the morning, my Lady Batten sent me a cart to carry away all my money, and plate, and best things, to Sir W. Rider's at Bednall-Greene. Which I did, riding myself in my night gown, in the cart; and, Lord! to see how the streets and the highways are crowded with people running and riding, and getting of carts at any rate to fetch away things. I find Sir W. Rider tired with being called up all night, and receiving things from several friends. His house full of goods, and much of Sir W. Batten's and Sir W. Pen's, I am eased at my heart to have my treasure so well secured. Then home, and with much ado to find a way, nor any sleep all this night to me nor my poor wife. Then all this day she and I, and all my people laboring to get away the rest of our things, and did get Mr. Tooker to get me a lighter to take them in, and we did carry them (myself some) over Tower Hill, which was by this time full of people's goods, bringing their goods thither; and down to the lighter, which lay at the next quay, above the Tower Dock. And here was my neighbor's wife…with her pretty child, and some few of her things, which I did willingly give way to be saved with mine; but there was no passing with anything through the postern the crowd was so great."

As is often the case in a crisis, some people began flooding into the area hoping to grab goods that were being left behind by others. In a similar vein, others realized they could charge top dollar to assist those evacuating with getting their property to safety. As the fire raged throughout September 3, there were actually more people in town than usual, as farmers and others flooded in from the countryside offering carts and strong backs for hire. Lady Hobert, who lived on Charncery Lane, wrote to a friend, "I am sorry to be the messenger of so dismal news. There was never so sad a sight, nor so doleful a cry heard, my heart is not able to express the tenth, nay, the thousandth part of it. . . . All the carts within ten miles round, and cars and drays, run about night and day and thousands of men and women carrying burdens. I am almost out of my wits. We have packed up all our goods and cannot get a cart for money, they give five and ten pounds for carts. I have sent for carts to my Lady Glascock if I can get them, but I fear I shall lose all I have and must run away. Oh, pray for us now, the cries make me I know not what to say, oh pity me. . . . Oh I shall lose all I have, we have sent to see for carts to send to Highgate and cannot get one for twenty pounds to go out of town."

In response to the panic and those seeking to capitalize off of it, the Duke of York, who was not only the king's brother but the chief constable of the city, took it upon himself to do what he could to keep order. According to Pepys, however, there was little he could do to quell domestic squabbles: "The Duke of York [came] this day by the office, and spoke to us, and did ride with his guard up and down the City to keep all quiet, (he being now General, and having the care of all). This day, Mercer being not at home, but against her mistress's order gone to her mother's, and my wife going thither to speak with W. Hewer, beat her there, and was angry; and her mother saying that she was not a 'prentice girl, to ask leave every time she goes abroad, my wife with good reason was angry, and when she come home bid her be gone again. And so she went away, which troubled me, but yet less than it would, because of the condition we are in, in fear of coming in a little time to being less able to keep one in her quality. At night lay down a little upon a quilt of W. Hewer's, in the office, all my own things being packed up or gone; and after me my poor wife did the like, we having fed upon the remains of yesterday's dinner, having no fire nor dishes, nor any opportunity of dressing anything."

By Monday afternoon, the crowds and the chaos had reached such a peak that the government officials in the city ordered the city's gates closed in an effort to provide greater motivation to fight the fire. One writer explained the rationale: "[While the gates were shut, that, no hopes of saving any things left, they might have more desperately endeavored the quenching of the fire." Not surprisingly, this plan didn't work any better than previous ones, and with that, King Charles II bypassed the authority of his Lord Mayor and put the Duke of York in charge of the city's efforts to fight the fire. One witness wrote, "The Duke of York and many of the nobility were as diligent as was possible. They commended and encouraged the forward, assisted the miserable sufferers and gave a most generous example to all by the vigorous opposition they made against the devouring flames." The same witness also noted that the Duke would "ride with his guard up and down the City to keep all quiet."

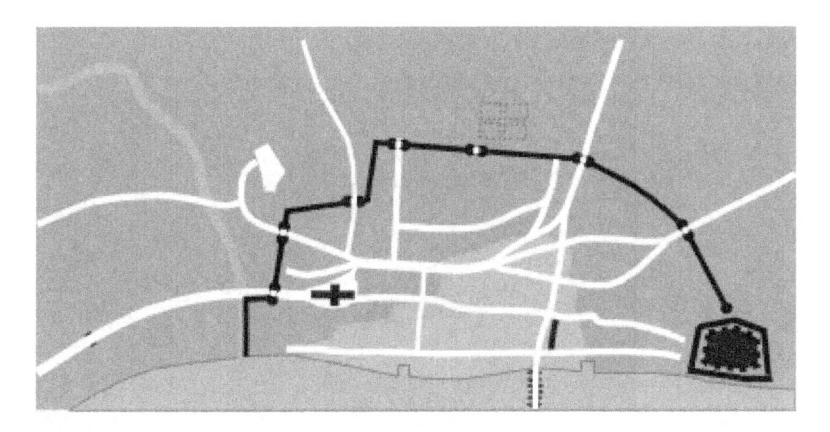

**The spread of the fire by the evening of September 3**

Since men were coming into the town to make money, the Duke used money from the royal coffers to hire them to fight the fire, primarily by tearing down buildings in its path. In order to make it clear under whose responsibility the houses were being destroyed, the Duke put his brother's most devoted courtiers in charge of those decisions, which freed anyone from feeling guilt for taking down a neighbor's home. John Evelyn was one of those courtiers and wrote about it in his diary: "It pleased his Majestie to command me among the rest to look after the quenching of fetter-lane end, to preserve (if possible) that part of Holborn, whilst the rest of the Gentlemen took their several posts, some at one part, some at another, for now they began to bestir themselves, and not 'til now, who 'til now had stood as men interdict, with their hands across, and began to consider that nothing was like to put a stop, but the blowing up of so many houses, as might make a [wider] gap, than any had yet been made by the ordinary method of pulling them down with Engines. This some stout Seamen proposed early enough to have saved the whole City. But some tenacious and avaricious Men, Aldermen, etcetera would not permit, because their houses must have been [of] the first. It was therefore now commanded to be practiced, and my concern being particularly for the Hospital of St. Bartholomew's near Smithfield, where I had many wounded and sick men, made me the more diligent to promote it; nor was my care for the Savoy less."

Someone later wrote of the Duke of York that he "hath won the hearts of the people with his continual and indefatigable pains day and night in helping to quench the fire, handing buckets of water with as much diligence as the poorest man that did assist; if the lord mayor had done as much his example might have gone far towards saving the city."

**Chapter 4: Members of the City**

**Lieve Verschuier's "The Great Fire of London in 1666"**

"Strangers, Dutch and French were, during the fire, apprehended, on suspicion that they contributed mischievously to it, who are all imprisoned, and Informations prepared to make a severe inquisition here upon by my Lord Chief Justice Keeling, assisted by some of the Lords of the Privy Council; and some principal Members of the City, notwithstanding which suspicion, the manner of the burning all along in a Train, and so blown forwards in all its ways by strong Winds, make us conclude that the whole was an effect of an unhappy chance, or to speak better, the heavy hand of God upon us for our sins, showing us the terror of his Judgement in thus raising the Fire, and immediately after his miraculous and never to be acknowledged Mercy, in putting a stop to it when we were in the last despair, and that all attempts for quenching it however industrially pursued seemed insufficient." - Excerpt from an article published in the *London Gazette* on September 11, 1666

As the day wore on, refugees from the fire continued to crowd the banks and waters of the Thames, making it nearly impossible for anyone to hire a boat to carry their possessions to safety. Evelyn observed, "Here we saw the Thames covered with goods floating, all the barges and boats laden with what some had time and courage to save, as on the other, the Carts and carrying out to the fields, which for many miles were strewed with moveables of all sorts, and Tents erecting to shelter both people and what goods they could get away. o the miserable and calamitous spectacle, such as happily the whole world had not seen the like since the foundation of it, nor to be out don, 'til the universal Conflagration of it, all the sky were of a fiery aspect, like the top of a burning Oven, and the light seen above 40 miles round about for many nights. God grant mine eyes may never behold the like, who now saw above ten thousand houses all in one flame, the noise and crackling and thunder of the impetuous flames, the shrieking of Women and children, the hurry of people, the fall of towers, houses and churches was like an hideous storm, and the air all about so hot and inflamed that at the last one was not able to approach it, so as they were forced [to] stand still, and let the flames consume on which they did for near two whole mile[s] in length and one in breadth. The Clouds also of Smoke were dismal, and reached upon computation near 50 miles in length. Thus I left it this afternoon burning, a resemblance of Sodom, or the last day. … London was, but is no more. Thus I returned."

Furthermore, rumors were spreading as fast as the flames, as people began trying to explain the disaster by blaming it on a scapegoat. Some claimed that the fires were being set by England's enemies in the Second Anglo-Dutch War, which was then raging, while others went as far as to speculate that the fires were actually being set in order to weaken the city and prepare it to be invaded. Since most of the newspaper offices in London were either on fire, in ashes, or in danger, there was no way to even try to inform the public of the truth, and eventually, the Coldstream Guards had to stop fighting the fire in order to keep violence against those under suspicion at bay.

Others blamed the Catholics living in the city, a charge that went back all the way to the Reformation more than a century earlier. In fact, just a few decades earlier, the English had beheaded King Charles II's own father, Charles I, in the process of setting up a government dominated by Puritans. As a result, those who still held to the traditional faith were often singled out for accusations. Indeed, a memorial erected to commemorate the fire included the following anti-Catholic allegation: "Here by permission of heaven, hell broke loose upon this Protestant city.....the most dreadful Burning of this City; begun and carried on by the treachery and malice of the Popish faction...Popish frenzy which wrought such horrors, is not yet quenched..."

In this case, the Catholics were accused of hiring a man named Robert Hubert to start the fires. Those who knew Hubert felt that he was mentally incompetent, but this was seen by his accusers as an asset, with one writing, "Tillotson, who believed the city was burnt on design, told me a circumstance that made the papists employing such a creased man in such service more credible. Langhorn, the popish counsellor at law, who for many years passed for a Protestant, was dispatching a half-witted man to manage the elections in Kent before the Restoration. Tillotson being present, and observing what a sort of a man he was, asked Langhorn how he could employ him in such service. Langhorn answered, it was a maxim with him in dangerous services to employ none but half-witted men, if they could but be secret and obey orders; for if they should change their minds and turn informers instead of agents, it would be easy to discredit them and to carry off the weight of any discoveries they could make and show they were madmen, and so not like to be trusted in critical things." In fact, Hubert did confess to starting the fire at one point, but his mental state was thought to be so unstable that no one paid any attention to him.

To his credit, one "foreigner" named Franciscus de Rapicani refused to hold a grudge against those that had accused him and instead praised those in London that day. He wrote, "It was indeed a pitiful sight, but the people's courage was so resilient, for the English are by nature not easily daunted, that it was not so much the loss caused by the dreadful fire that they were talking and worrying about as the war that they were waging on the sea against the Dutch."

**Chapter 5: About the Tower**

**A Victorian Era engraving depicting the fire**

"His Majesty then sat hourly in Council, and ever since has continued making rounds about the City in all parts of it where the danger and mischief was greatest, till the morning when he hath sent his Grace the Duke of Albermarle, whom he hath called for to assist him in this great occasion, to put his happy and successful hand to the finishing this memorable deliverance. About the Tower the seasonal orders given for plucking down the Houses to secure the Magazines of Powder was more especially successful, that part being up the Wind, notwithstanding which it came almost to the very Gates of it. So as by this early the general Stores of War lodged in the Tower were entirely saved: And we have further this intimate cause to give God thanks, that the fire did not happen where his Majesties Naval Stores are kept. So as though it had pleased God to visit us with his own hand, he hath not, by disfurnishing us with the means of carrying on the War, subjected us to our enemies." - Excerpt from an article published in the *London Gazette* on September 11, 1666

On Tuesday morning, September 4, the fire was burning worse than ever, and it even jumped the River Fleet, which the Duke and others had hoped would stop its advancement. Still, the Duke continued to act bravely, standing shoulder to shoulder with his men near the Fleet Bridge while any hope of stopping the conflagration remained. That said, people on the scene couldn't help but notice that there was little standing between the fire and the Palace of Whitehall, the king's main residence. As John Evelyn wrote a few hours later, "So as it pleased Almighty God by abating of the Wind, and the industry of people, now when all was lost, infusing a new Spirit into them (and such as had if exerted in time undoubtedly preserved the whole) that the fury of it began sensibly to abate, about noon, so as it came no farther than the Temple West-ward, nor than the entrance of Smithfield North; but continued all this day and night so impetuous toward Cripple-Gate, and The Tower, as made us even all despair. It also brake out again in the Temple: but the courage of the multitude persisting, and innumerable houses blown up with Gunpowder, such gaps and desolations were soon made, as also by the former three days consumption, as the back fire did not so vehemently urge upon the rest, as formerly."

**A 17th century illustration depicting the Palace of Whitehall**

Under the Duke of York's direction, it seemed that perhaps the fire would soon be put out, but when the wind kicked up again, it caused the flames to jump the firebreak he had had created to the north of the fire. At that point, it became obvious that the beautiful St. Paul's Cathedral was now in danger, even though it was previously the one place that everyone thought would surely be safe because of its thick stone walls. By Tuesday afternoon, it was completely full of refugees and goods from all the printers near the area, but the building was in the process of being remodeled and thus covered in very flammable wooden scaffolding. That proved to be just the tinder necessary to set every non-stone portion of the building ablaze. Evelyn wrote, "The burning still rages; I went now on horseback, and it was now gotten as far as the Inner Temple, all Fleete Streete, Old Bailey, Ludgate Hill, Warwick Lane, Newgate, Paules Chaine, Wattling-streete now flaming and most of it reduced to ashes, the stones of Paules flew like granados, the Lead melting down the streets in a stream, and the very pavements of them glowing with a fiery redness, so as nor horse nor man was able to tread on them, and the demolitions had stopped all the passages, so as no help could be applied; the Easter[n] Wind still more impetuously driving the flames forwards. Nothing but the almighty power of God was able to stop them, for vain was the help of man: …it crossed towards White-hall, but o the Confusion was then at that Court."

**A 17th century painting depicting the Great Fire burning Ludgate and Old St. Paul's**

## Cathedral

**A drawing depicting the burning of Old St. Paul's**

As the fire progressed on September 4, it was obvious that the fire was moving closer to Samuel Pepys' house on Seething Lane, but more importantly, it was also closing in on the Tower of London, where most of the city's gunpowder was stored. It was clear to everyone that should the fire reach the Tower of London, the resulting explosions would take much of the surrounding area with it. John Evelyn noted his concerns at this point: "I went this morning on foot from White hall as far as London bridge, through the Late Fleet Street, Ludgate Hill, by St. Paules, Cheape side, Exchange, Bishopsgate, Aldersgate, and out to Morefields, thence thro Cornehill, etcetera with extraordinary difficulty, clamoring over mountains of yet smoking rubbish, and frequently mistaking where I was, the ground under my feet so hot, as made me not only Sweat, but even burnt the soles of my shoes, and put me all over in Sweat. In the meantime his Majestie got to the Tower by Water, to demolish the houses about the Graft, which being built entirely about it, had they taken fire, and attacked the White Tower, where the Magazines of Powder lay, would undoubtedly have not only beaten down and destroyed all the bridge, but sunk and torn all the vessels in the river, and rendered the demolition beyond all expression for several miles even about the Country at many miles distance."

**Bob Collowan's picture of the Tower of London**

As Evelyn was caught up in the events that day, Pepys was busy from the beginning as well. He noted in his diary, "Up by break of day, to get away the remainder of my things; which I did by a lighter at the Iron Gate: and my hands so full, that it was the afternoon before we could get them all away. Sir W. Pen and I to the Tower-street, and there met the fire burning three or four doors beyond Mr. Howell's, whose goods, poor man, his trays, and dishes, shovels, etcetera, were flung all along Tower-street in the kennels, and people working therewith from one end to the other; the fire coming on in that narrow street, on both sides, with infinite fury. Sir W. Batten not knowing how to remove his wine, did dig a pit in the garden, and laid it in there; and I took the opportunity of laying all the papers of my office that I could not otherwise dispose of and in the evening Sir W. Pen and I did dig another, and put our wine in it; and I my parmesan cheese, as well as my wine and some other things."

At first, Pepys and others along the street hoped that the Duke of York might be able to send some help, but he was too overwhelmed to offer any help, so Pepys took matters into his own hands. He explained, "The Duke of York was at the office this day, at Sir W. Pen's; but I happened not to be within. This afternoon, sitting melancholy with Sir W. Pen in our garden, and thinking of the certain burning of this office, without extraordinary means, I did propose for the sending up of all our workmen from the Woolwich and Deptford yards, (none whereof yet appeared,) and to write to Sir W. Coventry to have the Duke of York's permission to pull down houses, rather than lose this office, which would much hinder the King's business. So Sir W. Pen went down this night, in order to the sending them up to-morrow morning; and I wrote to Sir W.

Coventry about the business, but received no answer."

Fortunately, the letter survived the fire itself and gives an insight into the agony and severity of the situation: "Sir,—The fire is now very near us as well on Tower Street as Fanchurch Street side, and we little hope of our escape but by that remedy, to the want whereof we do certainly owe the loss of the City, namely, the pulling down of houses, in the way of the fire. This way Sir W. Pen and myself have so far concluded upon the practicing, that he is gone to Woolwich and Deptford to supply himself with men and necessaries in order to the doing thereof, in case at his return our condition be not bettered and that he meets with [His Royal Highness'] approbation, which I have thus undertaken to learn of you, Pray please to let me have this night (at whatever hour it is) what [His Royal Highness'] directions are in this particular, Sir J. Minnes and Sir W. Batten having left us, we cannot add, though we are well assured of their, as well as all the neighborhoods' concurrence. Sir W.Coventry, Your obedient Servant, September. 4, 1666."

Pepys was also concerned for the safety and welfare of his neighbors, and he did what he could to comfort them. He wrote in his diary, "This night Mrs. Turner (who, poor woman, was removing her goods all this day, good goods into the garden, and knows not how to dispose of them) and her husband supped with my wife and me at night, in the office, upon a shoulder of mutton from the cook's, without any napkin, or anything, in a sad manner, but were merry. Only now and then, walking into the garden, saw how horribly the sky looks, all on a fire in the night, was enough to put us out of our wits; and, indeed, it was extremely dreadful, for it looks just as if it was at us, and the whole heaven on fire."

Following dinner, he again went out into the streets to monitor the fire's progress and that of those fighting it. He later described what he learned: "I after supper walked in the dark down to Tower-street, and there saw it all on fire, at the Trinity House on that side, and the Dolphin Tavern on this side, which was very near us; and the fire with extraordinary vehemence. Now begins the practice of blowing up of houses in Tower-street, those next the Tower, which at first did frighten people more than anything; but it stopped the fire where it was done, it bringing down the houses to the ground in the same places they stood, and then it was easy to quench what little fire was in it, though it kindled nothing almost. W. Hewer this day went to see how his mother did, and comes late home, telling us how he hath been forced to remove her to Islington, her house in Pye-corner being burned; so that the fire is got so far that way, and to the Old Bailey, and was running down to Fleet-street; and Paul's is burned, and all Cheepside. I wrote to my father this night, but the post-house being burned, the letter could not go."

**Chapter 6: We Began to Hope Well**

**Philip James de Loutherbourg's "The Great Fire of London" (1797)**

"By the favor of God the Wind slackened a little on Tuesday night and Flames meeting with brick buildings at the Temple, by little and little it was observed to lose its force on that side, so that on Wednesday morning we began to hope well, and his Royal Highness never despairing or slackening his personal care wrought so well that day, assisted in some parts by Lords of the Council before and behind is that a stop was put to it at the Temple Church, near Holborn-bridge, Pie-corner, Aldersgate, Cripple-gate, near the lower end of Coleman-street, at the end of Basin-hall-street by the Postern at the lower end of Bishopsgate-street and Leadenhall-street, at the Standard in Cornhill at the church in Fenchurch-street, near Cloth-workers Hall in Mincing-lane, at the middle of Mark-lane, and at the Tower-dock" - Excerpt from an article published in the *London Gazette* on September 11, 1666

As night fell on the evening of September 4, it seemed as though enough homes and other buildings had been destroyed to bring the fire under control. Thus, at one and the same time, Evelyn found himself saddened and relieved by what he had witnessed that day, and he wrote, "There was yet no standing near the burning and glowing ruins near a furlong's Space; The Coal and Wood wharves and magazines of oil, rosin, etcetera did infinite mischief; so as the invective I but a little before dedicated to his Majestie and published, giving warning what might probably be the issue of suffering those shops to be in the City, was looked on as prophetic. But there I left this smoking and sultry heap, which mounted up in dismal clouds night and day, the poor Inhabitants dispersed all about St. Georges, Moore fields, as far as highgate, and several miles in Circle, Some under tents, others under miserable Huts and Hovels, without a rag, or any necessary utensils, bed or board, who from delicateness, riches and easy accommodations in stately and well-furnished houses, were now reduced to extremist misery and poverty. In this Calamitous Condition I returned with a sad heart to my house, blessing and adoring the distinguishing mercy of God, to me and mine, who in the midst of all this ruin, was like Lot, in my little Zoar, safe and sound."

Pepys also noticed the wind dying down, which encouraged him enough to sleep, at least for awhile. Unfortunately, his rest was interrupted all too soon by another calamity that he described in his diary: "I lay down in the office again upon W. Hewer's quilt, being mighty weary, and sore in my feet with going till I was hardly able to stand. About two in the morning my wife calls me up, and tells me of new cries of fire, it being come to Barking Church, which is the bottom of our lane. I up; and finding it so, resolved presently to take her away, and did, and took my gold, which was about 2350 pounds. W. Hewer, and Jane, down by Proundy's boat to Woolwich; but Lord! What a sad sight it was by moon-light to see the whole City almost on fire, that you might see it plain at Woolwich, as if you were by it. There, when I come, I find the gates shut, but no guard kept at all; which troubled me, because of discourses now begun, that there is a plot in it, and that the French had done it. I got the gates open, and to Mr. Shelden's, where I locked up my gold, and charged my wife and W. Hewer never to leave the room without one of them in it, night or day. So back again, by the way seeing my goods well in the lighters at Deptford, and watched well by people. Home, and whereas I expected to have seen our house on fire, it being now about seven o'clock, it was not. But to the fire, and there find greater hopes than I expected; for my confidence of finding our office on fire was such, that I durst not ask anybody how it was with us, till I come and saw it was not burned."

In spite of all that had happened, Pepys was aware that progress was being made in halting the blaze, and he later recorded it with relief: "But going to the fire, I find by the blowing up of houses, and the great help given by the workmen out of the King's yards, sent up by Sir W. Pen, there is a good stop given to it, as well at Marke-lane end, as ours; it having only burned the dial of Barking Church, and part of the porch, and was there quenched. I up to the top of Barking steeple, and there saw the saddest sight of desolation that I ever saw; everywhere great fires, oil-cellars, and brimstone, and other things burning. I became afraid to stay there long, and therefore down again as fast as I could, the fire being spread as far as I could see it; and to Sir W. Pen's, and there eat a piece of cold meat…."

With some stability now coming, Pepys went about the town with some friends to try to determine what should be done next. He noted, "Here I met with Mr. Young and Whistler; and having removed all my things, and received good hopes that the fire at our end is stopped, they and I walked into the town, and find Fanchurch-street, Gracious-street, and Lumbard-street all in dust. The Exchange a sad sight, nothing standing there, of all the statues or pillars, but Sir Thomas Gresham's picture in the corner. Into Moore-fields, (our feet ready to burn, walking through the town among the hot coals,) and find that full of people, and poor wretches carrying their goods there, and everybody keeping his goods together by themselves; (and a great blessing it is to them that it is fair weather for them to keep abroad night and day;) drunk there, and paid two pence for a plain penny loaf. Thence homeward, having passed through Cheapside, and Newgate market, all burned; and seen Anthony Joyce's house in fire. And took up (which I keep by me) a piece of glass of Mercer's chapel in the street, where much more was, so melted and buckled with the heat of the fire like parchment. I also did see a poor cat taken out of a hole in a chimney, joining to the wall of the Exchange, with the hair all burned off the body, and yet alive."

**Chapter 7: Disaffection at Home**

"And we cannot but observe the confutation of all his Majesties enemies, who e:ndeavour to persuade the world abroad of great parties, and disaffection at home against his Majesties Government; that a greater instance of the affections of this City could never have been given than have now been given in this sad and deplorable Accident when if at any time disorder might have been expected from the losses, distraction, and almost desperation of some people in their private fortune, thousands of people not having had habitation to cover them. And yet in all this time it hath been so far from any appearance of designs or attempts against his Majesties Government, that his Majesty and his Royal Brother, out of their care to stop and prevent the fire, frequently exposing their persons with very small attendants in all parts of the Town-- sometimes even to be intermixed with those who labored in the business, yet never the less there have not been observed so much as a critical word to fall from any, but on the contrary, even those persons, whose losses rendered their conditions most desperate, and to be fit objects of others prayers, beholding those frequent instances of his Majesties care of his people, forgot their own misery, and filled the streets with their prayers for his Majesty, whose trouble they seemed to compassionate before their own." - Excerpt from an article published in the *London Gazette* on September 11, 1666.

People in London had already turned on scapegoats when the fire was reaching its peak, and as the fire began to come under control, a number of those suffering from exhaustion and taut nerves once again looked around for someone else to blame. Since the king and his court had performed so admirably during the crisis, they were spared serious recriminations, so the people who had lost so much turned their ire back to those living among them who had come to the city from other countries. Pepys heard about one riot breaking out near him and wrote in his diary, "So home at night, and find there good hopes of saving our office; but great endeavors of watching all night, and having men ready; and so we lodged them in the office, and had drink and bread and cheese for them. And I lay down and slept a good night about midnight: though when I rose, I heard that there had been a great alarm of French and Dutch being risen, which proved nothing. But it is a strange thing to see how long this time did look since Sunday, having been always full of variety of actions, and little sleep, that it looked like a week or more, and I had forgot almost the day of the week."

In fact, the "great alarm" Pepys referred to was a panic among those refugees housed on Parliament Hill and other nearby areas. Rumors began to spread that the city was in imminent danger of being attacked by 50,000 Dutch and French troops. Terrified and sleep deprived, many of those camping in the area rose up as an angry mob and attacked anyone they considered to be a foreigner. Evelyn explained, "[W]hen in the midst of all this Calamity and confusion, there was (I know not how) an Alarm begun, that the French and Dutch (with whom we were now in hostility) were not only landed, but even entering the City; there being in truth, great suspicion some days before, of those two nations joining, and even now, that they had been the occasion of firing the Town. This report did so terrify, that on a sudden there was such an uproar and tumult, that they ran from their goods, Taking what weapons they could come at, they could not be stopped from falling on some of those nations whom they casually met, without sense or reason, the clamor and peril growing so excessive, as made the whole Court amazed at it, and they did with infinite pains, and great difficulty reduce and appease the people, sending Guards and troops of soldiers, to cause them to retire into the fields again, where they were watched all this night when I left them pretty quiet, and came home to my house, sufficiently weary and broken. Their spirits thus a little sedated, and the affright abated, they now began to repair into the suburbs about the City, where such as had friends or opportunity got shelter and harbor for the Present; to which his Majesties Proclamation also invited them. Still the Plague, continuing in our parish, I could not without danger adventure to our Church."

A man named John Stewart also witnessed the sad fate of those from other countries who were caught in London at this time. He later recalled meeting "a man sadly bemoaning the great loss he was like to sustain, the fire then being within five or six houses of him. [He] did beseech the people, for God's sake, they having no goods of their own in danger to come in and help him to throw out trunks, chests, beds, etc , out at a window, having procured two carts or wagons to carry them away. Whereupon I ran into his house with several others, broke down his windows, threw out his goods and loaded the carts; and there being some interval of time before the return of the carts, and seeing a room wherein were many books and loose papers, which seemed to be a library, I went in and took down a book, which proved to be *Ovid's Metamorphoses*, and while I was looking upon it, there came into the same room an old man of a low stature with a white frock. . . I took him in my mind to be some groom come out of a stable. In the meantime there broke forth a fire among the papers which were behind us, there being none in the room but he and I. Whereupon the rest of the people . . . rushing in upon us, put out the fire with their feet. There was a small thing of a black matter, which looked like a piece of link burning, which questionless set fire on the papers, but was immediately trod out. [They] cried out we had set the room on fire, whereupon I took hold of the old man by the buttons under the throat and said 'How now, father, it must either be you or I that must fire these papers.'"

At that point, the situation was already heated, both literally and figuratively, and things soon got out of hand. Stewart continued, "He said 'Parce mihi, Domine.' The people, which did not understand it, cried out 'He is a Frenchman, kill him,' and with pulling of him, his periwig fell off. Then appeared a bald skull and under his frock, he had black clothes, I think of bishop's satin, whereupon he seemed to be a grave ecclesiastic person. I had much ado to save him from the people, but at last brought him before the Duke of York. We found in his pocket a bundle of papers closed up with wax like a packet, which was delivered to the Duke of York. I know not what was written in them, neither do I know what countryman he was, but I thought he looked something Jesuitical like. This I am certain of, that when I went into the room there was no fire in it, and it was fired when there was none but he and I in it, yet I cannot say I saw him do it, though I cannot but suspect he did it . . . because there were several houses untouched betwixt this house and where the fire was coming on . . . What became of this fellow after we had delivered him to his Royal Highness, the Duke of York, I have not heard."

To his credit, the king kept his head throughout the crisis. Concerned that civil unrest might lead to another Civil War, Charles II acted quickly and brought in food for people to alleviate the situation. Evelyn noted, "I then went towards Islington, and high-gate, where one might have seen two hundred thousand people of all ranks and degrees, dispersed, and laying along by their heaps of what they could save from the Incendium, deploring their loss, and though ready to perish for hunger and destitution, yet not asking one penny for relief, which to me appeared a stranger sight, than any I had yet beheld. His Majestie and Council indeed took all imaginable care for their relief, by Proclamation, for the Country to come in and refresh them with provisions…"

In the aftermath, The *London Gazette* also praised the king's response to the crisis: "Through this sad Accident it is easy to be imagined how many persons were necessitated to remove themselves and Goods into the open fields, where they were forced to continue some time, which could not but work compassion in the beholders, but his Majesties care was most signal in this occasion, who besides his personal pains was frequent in consulting all ways for relieving those distressed persons, which produced so good effect, as well as by his Majesties Proclamations and Orders issued to the Neighbors Justices of the Peace to encourage the sending in provisions to the Markets, which are publicly known, as by other directions, that when his Majesty, fearing lest other Orders might not have been sufficient, had commanded the Victualer of his Navy to send bread into the Moore-fields for relief of the poor, which for the more speedy supply he sent in biscuit out of the Sea Stores; it was found that the Markets had already been so well supplied that the people being un-accustomed to that kind of Bread declined it, and so it was returned in greater part to his Majesties Stores again without any use made of it."

**Chapter 8: Most Happily Mastered It**

"On Thursday by the blessing of God it was wholly beat down and extinguished. But so as that evening it unhappily burst out again a fresh at the Temple, by the falling of some sparks (as is supposed) upon a pile of wood buildings; but his Royal Highness who watched there that whole night in Person, by the great labours and diligence used, and especially by applying Powder to blow up the Houses about it, before day most happily mastered it." - Excerpt from an article published in the *London Gazette* on September 11, 1666.

With the fire dying down on Wednesday, September 5, Evelyn approached Charles on September 6 with an idea for how to best deal with some of the foreigners in the city. He explained, "Thursday, I represented to his Majestie the Case, of the French Prisoners at War in my Custody, and besought him, there might be still the same care of Watching at all places contiguous to unseized houses. It is not indeed imaginable how extraordinary the vigilance and activity of the King and Duke was, even laboring in person, and being present, to command, order, reward, and encourage Workemen; by which he showed his affection to his people, and gained theirs. Having then disposed of some under Cure, at the Savoy, I returned to white hall, where I dined at Mr. Offleys, Groome-porter, who was my relation, together with the Knight Martial, where I also lay that night."

Nevertheless, circumstances again conspired to make the fire seem like it was being set intentionally, because just as it was about finished, it seemingly started up again. This time, even Samuel Pepys was suspicious, as he noted in his diary: "Up about five o'clock; and met Mr. Gauden at the gate of the office, (I intending to go out, as I used, every now and then to-day, to see how the fire is,) to call our men to Bishop's-gate, where no fire had yet been near, and there is now one broke out: which did give great grounds to people, and to me too, to think that there is some kind of plot in this, (on which many by this time have been taken, and it hath been dangerous for any stranger to walk in the streets,) but I went with the men, and we did put it out in a little time; so that that was well again. It was pretty to see how hard the women did work in the cannels, sweeping of water; but then they would scold for drink, and be as drunk as devils. I saw good butts of sugar broke open in the street, and people give and take handfuls out, and put into beer, and drink it…"

With the situation again stabilized, Pepys was finally able to think about his own comfort: "[N]ow all being pretty well, I took boat, and over to Southwarke, and took boat on the other side the bridge, and so to Westminster, thinking to shift myself, being all in dirt from top to bottom; but could not there find any place to buy a shirt or a pair of gloves, Westminster Hall being full of people's goods, those in Westminster having removed all their goods, and the Exchequer money put into vessels to carry to Nonsuch but to the Swan, and there was trimmed: and then to White Hall, but saw nobody; and so home. … At home, did go with Sir W. Batten, and our neighbor, Knightly, (who, with one more, was the only man of any fashion left in all the neighborhood thereabouts, they all removing their goods, and leaving their houses to the mercy of the fire,) to Sir R. Ford's, and there dined in an earthen platter—a fried breast of mutton; a great many of us, but very merry, and indeed as good a meal, though as ugly a one, as ever I had in my life. Thence down to Deptford, and there with great satisfaction landed all my goods at Sir G. Carteret's safe, and nothing missed I could see or hear. This being done to my great content, I home, and to Sir W. Batten's, and there with Sir R. Ford, Mr. Knightly, and one Withers, a professed lying rogue, supped well, and mighty merry, and our fears over. From them to the office and there slept with the office full of laborers, who talked, and slept, and walked all night long there."

## Chapter 9: Very Great Loss

**The Londoners Lamentation, a popular broadside commemorating the fire**

**A depiction of surveyor Robert Hooke inspecting the damage**

"It must be observed, that this fire happened in a part of the Town, where though the commodities were not very rich, yet they were so bulky that they could not be well removed, so that the Inhabitants of that part where it first began have sustained very great loss, but the best enquiry we can make, the other parts of the Town where the commodities were of greater value, took the Alarum so early, that they saved most of their goods of value; which possibly may have diminished the loss. though some think that if the whole industry of the Inhabitants had been applied to the stopping of the fire, and not to the saving of their particular Goods, the success might have been much better, not only to the public, but to many of them in their own particulars." - Excerpt from an article published in the *London Gazette* on September 11, 1666.

Although the Great Fire of London is now recognized as burning out of control from September 2-5, it was not until Friday morning, September 7, that the conflagration was permanently put out. From there, all that was left was for Londoners to pick up the pieces. Pepys wrote on September 7, "Up by five o'clock; and, blessed be God! find all well; and by water to Pane's Wharf. Walked thence, and saw all the town burned, and a miserable sight of Paul's church, with all the roofs fallen, and the body of the quire fallen into St. Fayth's; Paul's school also, Ludgate, and Fleet-street. My father's house, and the church, and a good part of the Temple the like. So to Creed's lodging, near the New Exchange, and there find him laid down upon a bed; the house all unfurnished, there being fears of the fire's coming to them. There I borrowed a shirt of him, and washed. To Sir W. Coventry, at St. James's, who lay without curtains, having removed all his goods; as the King at White Hall, and everybody had done, and was doing."

Upon meeting with the king, Pepys discussed with him a concern on everyone's mind: the idea that the fire was deliberately set and that the city was in danger of invasion. He recorded the contents of this conversation: "He hopes we shall have no public distractions upon this fire, which is what everybody fears, because of the talk of the French having a hand in it. And it is a proper time for discontents; but all men's minds are full of care to protect themselves, and save their goods: the militia is in arms everywhere. Our fleets, he tells me, have been in sight one of another, and most unhappily by foul weather were parted, to our great loss, as in reason they do conclude; the Dutch being come out only to make a show, and please their people; but in very bad condition as to stores, victuals, and men. They are at Boulogne, and our fleet come to St. Ellen's. We have got nothing, but have lost one ship, but he knows not what. Thence to the Swan, and there drank; and so home, and find all well. My Lord Brouncker, at Sir W. Batten's, tells us the General is sent for up, to come to advise with the King about business at this juncture, and to keep all quiet; which is great honor to him, but I am sure is but a piece of dissimulation."

At the same time, after any great tragedy, there comes a point in which it's time to look forward, and Pepys felt this time had come by September 7. He wrote in his diary, "So home, and did give orders for my house to be made clean; and then down to Woolwich, and there find all well. Dined, and Mrs. Markham come to see my wife. This day our Merchants first met at Gresham College, which, by proclamation, is to be their Exchange. Strange to hear what is bid for houses; all up and down here; a friend of Sir W. Rider's having 150 pounds for what he used to let for 40 pounds per annum. Much dispute where the Custome-house shall be; thereby the growth of the City again to be foreseen. My Lord Treasurer, they say, and others, would have it at the other end of the town. I home late to Sir W. Pen's, who did give me a bed; but without curtains or hangings, all being down. So here I went the first time into a naked bed, only my drawers on; and did sleep pretty well: but still both sleeping and waking had a fear of fire in my heart, that I took little rest. People do all the world over cry out of the simplicity of my Lord Mayor in general; and more particularly in this business of the fire, laying it all upon him. A proclamation is come out for markets to be kept at Leadenhall and Mile-end-Greene, and several other places about the town; and Tower-hill, and all churches to be set open to receive poor people."

Meanwhile, Evelyn was making a survey of the city and its destruction on September 7. His first observation was of St. Paul's Cathedral, and he wrote sorrowfully in his diary for that day, "At my return I was infinitely concerned to find that goodly Church St. Paules now a sad ruin, and that beautiful Portico (for structure comparable to any in Europe, as not long before repaired by the late King) now rent in pieces, flakes of vast Stone Split in sunder, and nothing remaining entire but the Inscription in the Architrave which showing by whom it was built, had not one letter of it defaced: which I could not but take notice of. It was astonishing to see what immense stones the heat had in a manner Calcined, so as all the ornaments, Columns, freezes, Capitals and projectures of massive Portland stone flew off, even to the very roof, where a Sheet of Lead covering no less than 6 acres by measure, being totally melted, the ruins of the Vaulted roof, falling brake into St. Faiths, which being filled with the magazines of books, belonging to the Stationers, and carried thither for safety, they were all consumed burning for a week following. It is also observable, that the lead over the Altar at the East end was untouched; and among the…monuments, the body of one Bishop, remained entire."

Looking over the fallen walls, Evelyn was able to see down into the basements under the church and bemoaned all that had been lost: "Thus lay in ashes that most venerable Church, one of the Pieces of early Piety in the Christian world, beside near 100 more. The lead, ironwork, bells, plate all melted; the exquisitely wrought Mercers Chapel, the Sumptuous Exchange, the august fabric of Christ Church, all the rest of the Companies Halls, sumptuous buildings, Arches, Entries, all in dust. The fountains dried up and ruined, whilst the very waters remained boiling; the Voragos of subterranean Cellars Wells and Dungeons, formerly Warehouses, still burning in stench and dark clouds of smoke like hell, so as in five or six miles traversing about, I did not see one load of timber unconsumed, nor many stones but what were calcind white as snow, so as the people who now walked about the ruins, appeared like men in some dismal dessert, or rather in some great City, laid waste by an impetuous and cruel Enemy, to which was added the stench that came from some poor Creature's bodies, beds and other combustible goods."

**A contemporary sketch of the ruins of Old St. Paul's after the fire**

From St. Paul's, Evelyn continued touring the city, and in certain parts, he still saw some signs of life and noted a few of them in his diary. For example, he wrote that the "Sir Tho. Gresshams Statue, though fallen to the ground from its niche in the R. Exchange remained entire, when all those of the Kings since the Conquest were broken to pieces. Also the Standard in Cornhill, and Q. Elizabeth's Effigies, with some arms on Ludgate continued with but little detriment…"

Nonetheless, he was mostly overwhelmed by the sheer magnitude of the destruction: "[T]he vast iron Chains of the City streets, vast hinges, bars and gates of Prisons were many of them melted, and reduced to cinders by the vehement heats. Nor was I yet able to pass through any of the narrower streets, but kept [to] the widest, the ground and air, smoke and fiery vapor, continued so intense, my hair being almost singed, and my feet insufferably surbated. The by-lanes and narrower streets were quite filled up with rubbish, nor could one have possibly known where he was, but by the ruins of some church, or hall, that had some remarkable tower or pinnacle remaining."

After surveying the damage, Evelyn also quickly began looking forward. On September 10, he wrote, "I went again to the ruins, for it was now no longer a City." However, by September 13, he was discussing the coming rebuilding project: "Sat at Star Chamber, on the 13[th]. I presented his Majestie with a Survey of the ruins, and a Plot for a new City, with a discourse on it, whereupon, after dinner, his Majestie sent for me into the Queenes Bed-chamber, her Majestie and the Duke only present, where they examined each particular, and discoursed upon them for near a full hour, seeming to be extremely pleased with what I had so early thought on. The Queen was now in her Cavaliers riding habit, hat and feather and horseman's Coat, going to take the air; so I took leave of his Majestie and visiting the Duke of Albemarle, now newly returned from Sea, I went home."

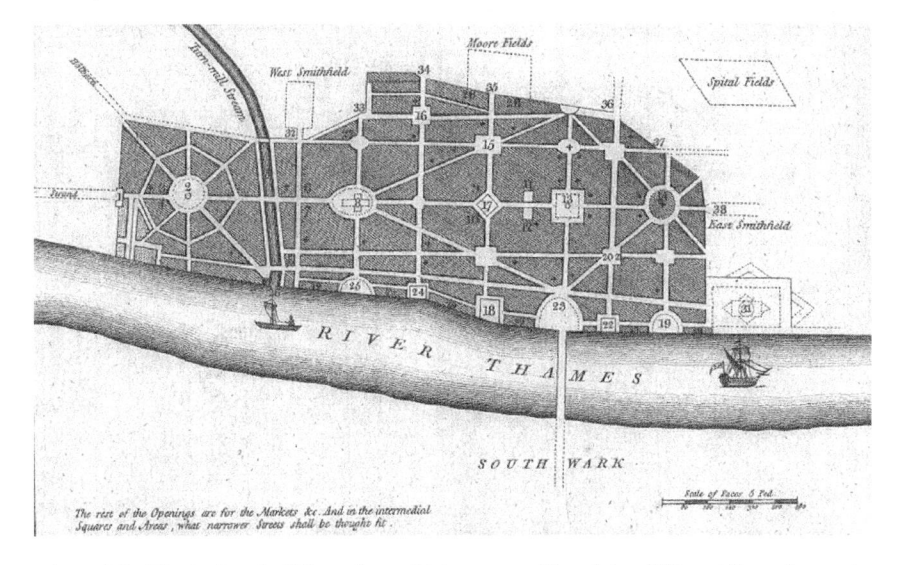

**A model of Evelyn's rebuilding plan, which was considered too different from the past road system to implement**

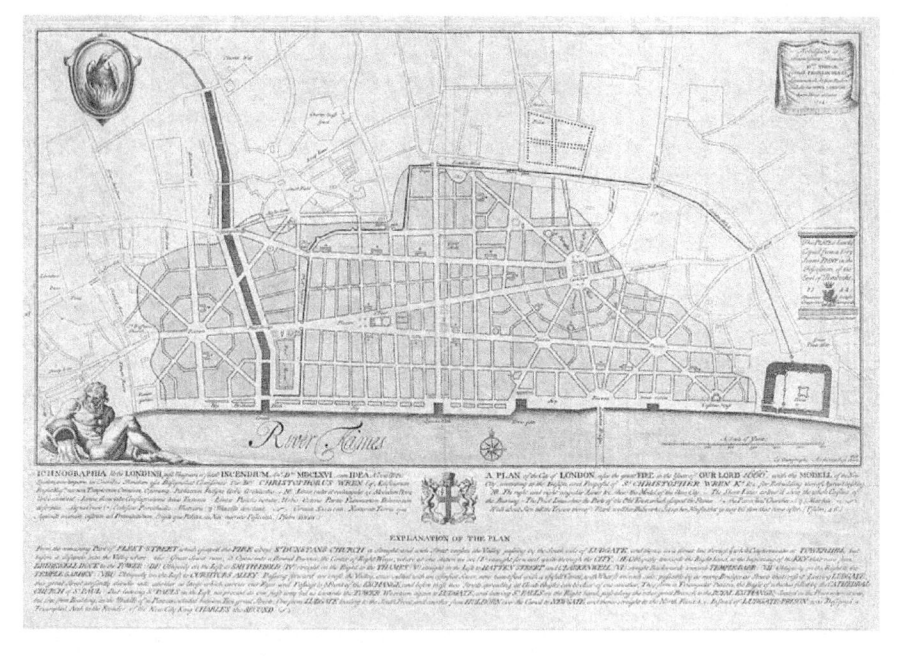

**Christopher Wren's proposed street system for rebuilding London**

Although Evelyn's plan for rebuilding London was ultimately not accepted, nobody could deny just how much work needed to be done. In all, it has been estimated that the fire destroyed nearly 15,000 houses, almost 90 churches, 44 Company Halls, the Royal Exchange, Old St. Paul's Cathedral, a number of prisons, and several of the city's gates as it spread west. All told, the property damage alone may have cost the modern equivalent of $1.5 billion, if not more.

On top of that, the kingdom initially intended to deal with all the assorted claims of ownership of houses that were destroyed and their previous locations while moving forward on a rebuilding plan. Its frustration in trying to sort that all out eventually gave way to abandoning such efforts, but in doing so, it had prevented more ambitious plans like Evelyn's from being used. As a result, London was ultimately rebuilt in much the same manner as it had stood on September 1, 1666.

**The monument commemorating the Great Fire of London**

**Online Resources**

Other books about English history by Charles River Editors

Other books about the Great Plague of London on Amazon

Other books about the Great Fire of London on Amazon

**Bibliography**

Contributors, Harvard University Library. "The Great Plague of London, 1665." *Harvard University Library*. The President and Fellows of Harvard College, 2008. Web. 27 Mar. 2017. <http://ocp.hul.harvard.edu/contagion/plague.html>.

Ross, David. "The London Plague of 1665." *The London Plague of 1665*. David Ross, 2010. Web. 27 Mar. 2017. <http://www.britainexpress.com/History/plague.htm>.

Editors, UK National Archives. "Great Plague of 1665-1666." *The National Archives*. The National Archives Kew, Richmond, Surrey, 2015. Web. 27 Mar. 2017. <http://www.nationalarchives.gov.uk/education/resources/great-plague/>.

Stanbridge, Nicola. "DNA confirms cause of 1665 London's Great Plague." *BBC News*. BBC, 8 Sept. 2016. Web. 27 Mar. 2017. <http://www.bbc.com/news/science-environment-37287715>.

Fenn, Chris, Katy Stoddard, Apple Chan-Fardel, and Paul Torpey. "Mapping London's great plague of 1665." *The Guardian*. Guardian News and Media, Ltd., 12 Aug. 2015. Web. 27 Mar. 2017. <https://www.theguardian.com/society/ng-interactive/2015/aug/12/london-great-plague-1665-bills-of-mortality>.

Editors, BBC. "The Great Plague." *BBC Bitesize*. BBC, 2016. Web. 27 Mar. 2017. <http://www.bbc.co.uk/education/guides/zd3wxnb/revision/2>.

Authors, Snopes. "Ring Around the Rosie." *Snopes*. Proper Media, 12 July 2015. Web. 27 Mar. 2017. <http://www.snopes.com/language/literary/rosie.asp>.

Smallwood, Karl. "TOADS AROUND YOUR NECK AND FORCING KIDS TO SMOKE- ESCAPING THE GREAT PLAGUE OF LONDON (1665-1666)." *Today I Found Out*. Today I Found Out, 27 May 2015. Web. 27 Mar. 2017. <http://www.todayifoundout.com/index.php/2015/05/great-plague-london/>.

Authors, The Black Death. "How does the nursery rhyme "Ring around the Rosie" Relate to the Black Death?" *The Black Death*. Blogspot, 17 May 2011. Web. 27 Mar. 2017. <http://theblackdeathkc.blogspot.tw/2011/05/how-does-nursery-rhyme-ring-around.html>.

Schladweiler, Jon. "The history of a nursery rhyme — Ring around the Rosie." *The History of Sanitary Sewers*. WordPress, 19 Feb. 2002. Web. 27 Mar. 2017. <http://www.sewerhistory.org/miscellaneous/the-history-of-a-nursery-rhyme-ring-around-the-

rosie/>.

Benedictow, Ole J. "The Black Death: The Greatest Catastrophe Ever." *History Today*. History Today, Ltd., 3 Mar. 2005. Web. 27 Mar. 2017. <http://www.historytoday.com/ole-j-benedictow/black-death-greatest-catastrophe-ever>.

Stöppler, Melissa Conrad, MD. "Plague (Black Death)." *MedicineNet*. Ed. Steven Doerr. MedicineNet, Inc., 8 Oct. 2015. Web. 27 Mar. 2017. <http://www.medicinenet.com/plague_facts/article.htm>.

Editors, Healthline. "The Plague." *Healthline*. Healthline Media, 2016. Web. 27 Mar. 2017. <http://www.healthline.com/health/plague#Overview1>.

Authors, History Channel. "BLACK DEATH." *History Channel*. A&E Television Networks, LLC, 2015. Web. 27 Mar. 2017. <http://www.history.com/topics/black-death>.

Snell, Melissa. "The Spread of the Black Death through Europe." *Thought Company*. About, Inc., 13 Jan. 2017. Web. 27 Mar. 2017. <https://www.thoughtco.com/spread-of-the-black-death-through-europe-4123214>.

Hope, Jessica. "10 things you (probably) didn't know about the Black Death." *History Extra*. Immediate Media Company, 2 Nov. 2015. Web. 27 Mar. 2017. <http://www.historyextra.com/article/international-history/10-things-you-probably-didnt-know-about-black-death>.

Newman, Simon. "The Black Death." *The Finer Times*. The Finer Times, 8 Oct. 2014. Web. 28 Mar. 2017. <http://www.thefinertimes.com/Middle-Ages/the-black-death.html>.

Wheelis, Mark. "Biological Warfare at the 1346 Siege of Caffa." *Centers for Disease Control and Prevention*. CDC Media, 16 July 2010. Web. 28 Mar. 2017. <https://wwwnc.cdc.gov/eid/article/8/9/01-0536_article>.

Steve, Rick. "The Plague That Shook Medieval Europe." *Rick Steve's Europe*. Rick Steves' Europe, Inc., 2017. Web. 28 Mar. 2017. <https://www.ricksteves.com/watch-read-listen/read/articles/the-plague-that-shook-medieval-europe>.

Editors, SHSU. "Boccaccio describes the Plague in Florence in the Introduction of the Decameron." *Sam Houston State University*. Sam Houston State University, 2003. Web. 28 Mar. 2017. <http://www.shsu.edu/~his_ncp/Boccaccio.html>.

Pearce, Ian. "Black Death." *Great Ayton*. Great Ayton, May 2009. Web. 28 Mar. 2017. <http://greatayton.wdfiles.com/local--files/public-health/Black-Death.pdf>.

Editors, AF. "The plague in Milan." *Archivum Fabricae*. Veneranda Fabbrica del Duomo di Milano, Feb. 2015. Web. 28 Mar. 2017. <http://archivio.duomomilano.it/en/infopage/the-plague-in-milan/bfa2bcc5-5bbc-4729-9181-46f6646bece7/>.

Authors, Museum of London. "London Plagues 1348-1665." *Museum of London*. Museum of London, 2013. Web. 28 Mar. 2017. <https://www.museumoflondon.org.uk/application/files/5014/5434/6066/london-plagues-1348-1665.pdf>.

Williams, Chris. "ANATOMY OF A FLEA BITE." *Colonial Pest Control*. Colonial Pest Control, Inc., 11 Sept. 2014. Web. 28 Mar. 2017. <http://www.colonialpest.com/anatomy-of-a-flea-bite/>.

Authors, Sunday Times. "The novice's study." *Sunday Times*. Wijeya Newspapers, Ltd., 2006. Web. 28 Mar. 2017. <http://www.sundaytimes.lk/060702/plus/PlusP4.1.html>.

Editors, Stone Age Refugee. "How many valiant men..." *Stone Age Refugee*. WordPress, 24 Mar. 2011. Web. 28 Mar. 2017. <https://stoneagerefugee.wordpress.com/2011/03/24/how-many-valiant-men-how-many-fair-ladies-breakfast-with-their-kinfolk-and-the-same-night-supped-with-their-ancestors-in-the-next-world-the-condition-of-the-people-was-pitiable-to-behold-they-sick/>.

Frith, John. "The History of Plague – Part 1. The Three Great Pandemics." *Journal of Military and Veterans' Health*. Australasian Military Medicine Association, 4 Feb. 2012. Web. 28 Mar. 2017. <http://jmvh.org/article/the-history-of-plague-part-1-the-three-great-pandemics/>.

DNews. "Bubonic Plague Originated in China." *Seeker*. Group Nine Media, 1 Nov. 2010. Web. 28 Mar. 2017. <https://www.seeker.com/bubonic-plague-originated-in-china-1765135886.html>.

Walker, Cameron. "Bubonic Plague Traced to Ancient Egypt." *National Geographic News*. National Geographic Society, 10 Mar. 2004. Web. 28 Mar. 2017. <http://news.nationalgeographic.com/news/2004/03/0310_040310_blackdeath.html>.

Authors, Telegraph. "Medieval London: 10 disgusting facts." *The Telegraph*. Telegraph Media Group, Ltd., 5 Apr. 2011. Web. 29 Mar. 2017. <http://www.telegraph.co.uk/culture/tvandradio/8421415/Medieval-London-10-disgusting-facts.html>.

Kollenborn, K. P. "15 Medieval Hygiene Practices That Might Make You Queasy." *K.P.Kollenborn*. Blogspot, 9 Jan. 2015. Web. 29 Mar. 2017. <http://kpkollenborn.blogspot.tw/2014/11/15-medieval-hygiene-practices-that.html>.

Richter, Ash M. "13 Gross Medieval Hygiene Practices That Will Give You Nightmares." *All Day*. All Day, 2015. Web. 29 Mar. 2017. <http://www.allday.com/13-gross-medieval-hygiene-practices-that-will-give-you-nightmares-2180807051.html>.

Authors, GSSG. "Life in a Medieval Town." *Go Social Studies Go*. Wix, 2008. Web. 29 Mar. 2017. <http://www.gohistorygo.com/medieval-towns->.

Brown, Stephanie. "What did medieval people think caused the Black Death, and how did they respond accordingly?" *Gorffennol Student Journal*. British Conference of Undergraduate Research, Winter 2007. Web. 29 Mar. 2017. <http://gorffennol.swansea.ac.uk/wp-content/uploads/2016/01/2-Black-Death.pdf>.

Banks-Smith, Nancy. "Dead reckoning ." *The Guardian*. Guardian News and Media, Ltd., 16 Oct. 2001. Web. 29 Mar. 2017. <https://www.theguardian.com/media/2001/oct/16/tvandradio.television1>.

Conlon, Katherine. "The Plague Pits of London." *Travel Darkly*. Travel Darkly, Ltd., 23 Apr. 2014. Web. 29 Mar. 2017. <http://www.traveldarkly.com/plague-pits-london/>.

Editors, Encyclopedia.Com. "Bills Of Mortality." *Encyclopedia.Com*. The Gale Group, Inc., 2002. Web. 30 Mar. 2017. <http://www.encyclopedia.com/history/modern-europe/british-and-irish-history/bills-mortality>.

Johnson, Ben. "The Great Plague." *Historic UK*. Historic UK, Ltd., 4 Jan. 2013. Web. 30 Mar. 2017. <http://www.historic-uk.com/HistoryUK/HistoryofEngland/The-Great-Plague/>.

Mason, Emma. "London's 7 most memorable lord mayors." *History Extra*. Immediate Media Company, 5 Sept. 2016. Web. 30 Mar. 2017. <http://www.historyextra.com/article/feature/london-lord-mayors-history-7-most-memorable>.

Trueman, C. N. "The Lord Mayor's Orders." *The History Learning Site*. The History Learning Site, Ltd., 17 Mar. 2015. Web. 30 Mar. 2017. <http://www.historylearningsite.co.uk/stuart-england/the-lord-mayors-orders/>.

Trueman, C. N. "Eyam and the Great Plague of 1665." *The History Learning Site*. The History Learning Site, Ltd., 16 Aug. 2016. Web. 30 Mar. 2017. <http://www.historylearningsite.co.uk/stuart-england/eyam-and-the-great-plague-of-1665/>.

Staff, Mayo Clinic. "Symptoms and causes." *Mayo Clinic*. Mayo Foundation for Medical Education and Research, 15 Mar. 2016. Web. 30 Mar. 2017. <http://www.mayoclinic.org/diseases-conditions/plague/symptoms-causes/dxc-20196766>.

White, Frances. "Why did doctors during the Black Death wear 'beak masks'?" *History

*Answers*. Imagine Publishing Media, 2 June 2014. Web. 30 Mar. 2017. <https://www.historyanswers.co.uk/people-politics/why-did-doctors-during-the-black-death-wear-beak-masks/>.

Birkwood, Katie. "For the cure of the plague." *Royal College of Physicians*. The Royal College of Physicians of London, 15 May 2015. Web. 30 Mar. 2017. <https://www.rcplondon.ac.uk/news/cure-plague>.

Editors, RCP. "Plague remedies from the garden." *Royal College of Physicians*. The Royal College of Physicians of London, 4 Aug. 2015. Web. 30 Mar. 2017. <https://www.rcplondon.ac.uk/news/plague-remedies-garden>.

Smith, Lisa. "Tag: Pest House Fields." *The Sloane Letters Project*. University of Saskatchewan , 15 Mar. 2013. Web. 30 Mar. 2017. <http://sloaneletters.com/tag/pest-house-fields/>.

Shariff, Mohammed. "10 Crazy Cures for the Black Death." *Listverse*. Listverse, Ltd., 21 Jan. 2013. Web. 31 Mar. 2017. <http://listverse.com/2013/01/21/10-crazy-cures-for-the-black-death/>.

Johnson, Ben. "The Great Fire of London." *Historic UK*. Historic UK, Ltd., 3 Sept. 2016. Web. 31 Mar. 2017. <http://www.historic-uk.com/HistoryUK/HistoryofEngland/The-Great-Fire-of-London/>.

Authors, The Week. "What was Black Death and how did it end?" *The Week*. The Week, Ltd., 31 Aug. 2016. Web. 31 Mar. 2017. <http://www.theweek.co.uk/76088/what-was-black-death-and-how-did-it-end>.

Morelle, Rebecca. "'Gerbils replace rats' as main cause of Black Death." *BBC News*. BBC, 24 Feb. 2015. Web. 31 Mar. 2017. <http://www.bbc.com/news/science-environment-31588671>.

Editors, Wikipedia. "Theories of the Black Death." *Wikpedia*. Wikimedia Foundation, Inc., 1 Mar. 2017. Web. 31 Mar. 2017. <https://en.wikipedia.org/wiki/Theories_of_the_Black_Death#Ebola-like_virus>.

Creighton, Charles. *A History of Epidemics in Britain: From AD 664 to the Extinction of Plague*. Vol. 1. N.p.: Cambridge U Press, 2013. Print.

Hughes, Robert. *Barcelona*. N.p.: Vintage, 1993. Print.

Gill, John. *Andalucia: A Cultural History (Landscapes of the Imagination)*. N.p.: Oxford U Press, 2008. Print.

Porter, Stephen. *The Great Plague*. N.p.: Sutton Pub Ltd, 2000. Print.

Hays, Jo N. *Epidemics and Pandemics: Their Impacts on Human History*. 1st ed. N.p.: ABC-CLIO, 2005. Print.

Stone, Jon R. *The Routledge Dictionary of Latin Quotations: The Illiterati's Guide to Latin Maxims, Mottoes, Proverbs, and Sayings (Latin for the Illiterati)*. Bilingual ed. N.p.: Routledge, 2004. Print.

Gaskill, Malcolm. *Witchfinders: A Seventeenth-Century English Tragedy*. N.p.: Harvard U Press, 2007. Print.

Jones, Becky, and Clare Lewis. *The Bumper Book of London: Everything You Need to Know About London and More...* . N.p.: Frances Lincoln, 2012. Print.

Moote, A. Lloyd, and Dorothy C. Moote. *The Great Plague: The Story of London's Most Deadly Year* . 1st ed. N.p.: Johns Hopkins U Press, 2006. Print.

Wright, Cindy. *The Dark Traveller*. N.p.: Lulu.Com, 2012. Print.

Withington, John. *London's Disasters: From Boudicca to the Banking Crisis*. N.p.: The History Press, 2010. Print.

Hayden, Deborah. *Pox: Genius, Madness, And The Mysteries Of Syphilis*. Reprint ed. N.p.: Basic , 2003. Print.

Hyde, Edward. *The History of the Rebellion and Civil Wars in England Begun in the Year 1641: (History of the Rebellion & Civil Wars in England Begun in the Year 1641)* . Ed. W. Dunn Macray. Vol. 5. N.p.: Clarendon Press, 1993. Print.

Appleby, Andrew B. *The Disappearance of Plague: A Continuing Puzzle*. N.p.: Economic History Society, 1980. Print.

N.p. "The Great Plague." *Plague, Fire, War and Treason: A Century of Troubles*. Channel 4. London, 31 Oct. 2005. Television.

Oliver, Dan. "Secrets of the Great Plague ." *Secrets of the Great Plague*. Dir. Tom Pollock. Atlantic Productions See. 28 Aug. 2006. Television.

Evelyn, John (1854). *Diary and Correspondence of John Evelyn, F.R.S.* London: Hurst and Blackett. Retrieved 5 November 2006.

Hanson, Neil (2001). *The Dreadful Judgement: The True Story of the Great Fire of London*. New York: Doubleday.

Hanson, Neil (2002). *The Great Fire of London: In That Apocalyptic Year, 1666*. Hoboken, New Jersey: John Wiley and Sons.

Leasor, James (1961, 2011). *The Plague and the Fire*.

Morgan, Kenneth O. (2000). *Oxford Illustrated History of Britain*. Oxford: Oxford.

Pepys, Samuel (1995). Robert Latham and William Matthews (eds.), ed. *The Diary of Samuel Pepys, Vol. 7*. London: Harper Collins.

Tinniswood, Adrian (2003). *By Permission of Heaven: The Story of the Great Fire of London*. London: Jonathan Cape.

## Free Books by Charles River Editors

We have brand new titles available for free most days of the week. To see which of our titles are currently free, click on this link.

## Discounted Books by Charles River Editors

We have titles at a discount price of just 99 cents everyday. To see which of our titles are currently 99 cents, click on this link.

Printed in Great Britain
by Amazon